Settled Accounts

Learning how to Forgive and Release

Joff Day

Sovereign World

Sovereign World Ltd
P0 Box 777
Tonbridge
Kent TX11 9XT
England

ISBN: 1–85240–138–9

Typeset by CRB (Drayton) Typesetting Services, Norwich.
Printed in England by Clays Ltd, St. Ives plc.

Contents

Foreword

The central foundation of this book is the belief that the Cross of Christ made reconciliation between God and man possible. Not only that, but it also made reconciliation between man and man possible.

The only hope for this war-torn world is what Christ accomplished through His death and resurrection.

It is He who broke down the barriers that divide (Ephesians 2:14).

It is He that takes Jew and Gentile, black and white, Catholic and Protestant, slave and free, parent and child and baptises them into one Body. That Body, His Church, is to demonstrate to the world that all distinctions of race, colour and culture are no longer barriers to friendship and peace.

He is the one that came to bind the brokenhearted. He is the one that came to set the captives free. That work did not end at His ascension. He commissioned His followers to take the good news of the 'favourable year of the Lord' to every nation.

Forgiveness – biblical forgiveness – is the theme of this book. Forgiveness is not a rational exercise to clear the mind and justify the conscience. Nor is it merely an emotional enema. It is the application of the work of the Cross in our lives. We can have mercy on and release all those who have sinned against us, **because** we, ourselves, have been forgiven and released.

Introduction

Why forgive and release? I am using these two words to convey one biblical concept – forgiveness. Jesus taught clearly that to forgive is also to release.

Sadly, there are many Christians who do not understand this. Some have been taught by well meaning leaders that even though they may have forgiven someone for an issue, if they are still hurting over the issue, they will have to forgive them again and again (for the same issue) until the hurt finally disappears.

If Jesus' teaching on forgiveness was to be understood correctly, they would see that they had not forgiven 'from their heart' in the first place. They may have made a mental decision to 'forgive', but their heart had not 'released' the offender from the debt. That is why they still hurt concerning the issue.

There is much hurt and mistrust in the Body of Christ today. Some of it lingers on because the principles of forgiveness have not been fully understood. This book seeks to explain forgiveness, not create a 'forgiveness plus...' gospel.

For many people I have spoken to, understanding forgiveness as 'forgiving and releasing', has helped them resolve many unresolved hurts from their past, and come into a new freedom in Christ. It has also helped them make a commitment for the future to forgive as Jesus taught, whatever circumstances come their way.

If you have ever had cause to forgive anyone or think you may need to now or in the future, then this book is for you.

Chapter 1

A Wounded Heart

When I looked at the wound on the top of my leg, my stomach turned. There was a gaping hole, exposing pusy infected flesh. The wound was about 8 inches long and the edges were red and inflamed. God then spoke to me.

'If you will forgive and release Sue (not her real name), then I will heal the wound.'

The question I had was 'After what she's done, how can I?' I felt owed. I had given what I thought a steady relationship like ours required. I really did love her. I thought I had done everything to be faithful to her, but now she had jilted me, with no real explanation. I was hurt and disappointed.

She had been on fire for God once. There were times when I had been totally intimidated by her boldness and confidence. Recently her walk with God had grown cold. A move in her job gave her the opportunity to make new friends and a new start. It also gave her the chance to finish with me and go out with someone else she had found.

Now every time I thought of her I felt sick in the pit of my stomach. When I heard people talking about her or mentioning her name, I winced. When I saw her it was worse! As the weeks went on, the pain did not decrease. The old adage 'Time is a good healer' seemed to be a load of rubbish. Now God was asking me to forgive her.

It was Capel Bible Week. One of the speakers had told us to go and get things sorted out where relationships were wrong in our lives. It was a beautiful hot summer's day so I went into a marquee to pray. As I started to pray, I had a vision (or some form of picture) of the top of my leg. I was wearing shorts, so the picture seemed vivid and real. In the vision I saw a wound on my leg. I could easily see how it was like the wound I felt in my heart. Then the Lord showed me that whenever I thought about this person I had loved, the devil took a knife and dug it in the flesh. The pain was excruciating, the sense of unfairness overwhelming.

I could bear it no longer. I forgave her and released her from all that I sensed she owed me. I also asked God to forgive me for being bitter and jealous. As I did this, I saw a hand come down over the wound on my leg. As it passed over the top of my leg, the wound vanished.

'What do you see?' came the voice again. 'New flesh,' I replied. 'Touch it' the voice said. I touched my leg. There was no pain, but it was sensitive to touch. 'There is no scar. Your emotions are whole again, and you can be hurt again.' At that moment, I knew that I had settled accounts that had been outstanding. God had graciously forgiven me too, and inexplicably brought healing to my heart.

When I saw or spoke to Sue after that, I couldn't believe how I felt. No anger, no jealousy, no resentment. It was wonderful.

Chapter 2

Roots, Fruit, Seeds and Soil

About ten years later while meditating on the issues of forgiveness, God started to teach me afresh about what really happened to me in that marquee at Capel. He showed me another picture, which, I trust, will help you settle accounts once and for all with those who have hurt you.

Your experience is probably like mine in that most people you meet who grumble, complain, gossip or in any way speak negatively, are hurting on the inside. There's a number of options when you have been hurt. One is to continually mull over the situation in your mind, and let the hurt get worse.

Another option is to bury the hurt and build up defence mechanisms on the inside, both mentally and emotionally. These thought patterns (strongholds) promise to protect you from getting hurt again. e.g., 'I'll never get involved with a woman again.' 'He let me down badly. I'll never do business with his sort again.' Rationally these defences make sense. But that which is built up to defend, quickly becomes a stronghold that imprisons.

Another option is to get even! You deal with the people who have hurt you by hurting them. When you are really hurt, you try to hurt the other people before they get a chance to hurt you. That is what often happens in marriages that are struggling. One partner will try to hurt the other because they don't want to get hurt themselves

However, the bottom line on all these options is that on the inside, a person gets bitter. God's heart is that we don't get bitter, we get better. That's the Christian option. You don't stay hurt, you get healed.

Let's look at some scriptures concerning bitterness:

In Deuteronomy 29, Moses spells out the terms of the covenant that God was making with His people. He commands them to avoid the idolatry of other nations.

> *'... lest there shall be among you a man or woman, or family or tribe, whose heart turns away today from the Lord our God, to go and serve the gods of those nations; lest there shall be among you a root bearing poisonous fruit and wormwood. And it shall be when he hears the words of this curse, that he will boast, saying, "I have peace though I walk in the stubbornness of my heart in order to destroy the watered land with the dry." The Lord shall never be willing to forgive him, but rather the anger of the Lord and His jealousy will burn against that man, and every curse which is written in this book will rest on him, and the Lord will blot out his name from under heaven. Then the Lord will single him out for adversity from all the tribes of Israel, according to all the curses of the covenant which are written in this book of the law.'*
>
> (Deuteronomy 29:18–21)

The writer to the Hebrews picks up on the aspect of bitterness.

> *'See to it that no one comes short of the grace of God; that no root of bitterness springing up causes trouble, and by it many be defiled.'* (Hebrews 12:15)

Let us consider some of the phrases of these verses and see if God's response to bitterness of heart is the same under the New Covenant as the Old.

The Bible has a lot to say about roots, fruit, seeds and soil. As the picture below develops, we will see how we get hurt emotionally and the effect it can have on our lives.

```
┌─────────────────────────────────────────┐
│                                           │
│                            Fruit          │
│                                           │
│         Seed                              │
│                                           │
│                                           │
│  ≈≈≈≈≈≈≈≈≈≈≈≈≈≈≈≈≈≈≈≈≈≈≈≈≈≈≈≈≈≈≈≈≈≈≈≈    │
│  Soil                                     │
│                                           │
│                        Root               │
│                                           │
└─────────────────────────────────────────┘
```

Deuteronomy 29:15 talks about a
   root
   bearing poisonous fruit
Hebrews 12:15 says the root
   springs up
   causing trouble
   defiles many
Deuteronomy 29:19 says it's to do with
   stubbornness of heart
Let's now read what God's response is to this kind of person.

> *'The Lord shall never be willing to forgive him, but rather the anger of the Lord and His jealousy will burn against that man, and every curse which is written in this book will rest on him, and the Lord will blot out his name from under heaven. Then the Lord will single him out for adversity.'* (Deuteronomy 29:20f)

As Christians, we rejoice that Christ has redeemed us from the curse of the law.

> *'Christ redeemed us from the curse of the law by becoming a curse for us, for it is written: "Cursed is everyone who is hung on a tree."'* (Galatians 3:13)

But is there any way that under the New Covenant we might open ourselves up to the curses? If there is a root of bitterness within us, there is likely to be fruit of it in our lives. Would God lift His hand of blessing from our lives if we are like this? I believe He does.

We are going to see that as a result of the soil of insecurity within our lives, seeds of offence take root and bear poisonous fruit. Mental, emotional and physical sicknesses and afflictions are often the result.

However the good news is that God has provided a way to reverse the curse, dig out the roots and provide us with internal security. First we need to understand the principles of forgiveness.

Chapter 3

Debts and Debtors

Matthew, chapters 5–7, have been rightly described as the 'Manifesto of the Kingdom.' Here, Jesus spells out practically what life is like for citizens of the Kingdom of God. Living under the government of God, with Jesus as King, has implications.

> *'Pray, then, in this way: "Our Father who art in heaven, Hallowed be Thy name. Thy kingdom come. Thy will be done, On earth as it is in heaven. Give us this day our daily bread. And forgive us our debts, as we also have forgiven our debtors. And do not lead us into temptation, but deliver us from evil."*
>
> *For if you forgive men for their transgressions, your heavenly Father will also forgive you. But if you do not forgive men, then your Father will not forgive your transgressions.'* (Matthew 6:9–15)

The sense behind the word **debt** is 'that which is legally due'.

The sense behind the word **debtor** is 'one that has not yet made amends to one whom he has injured'.

Jesus makes it very clear in these verses that if we don't forgive, then God will not forgive us. He is talking about life under the New Covenant here, not the Old. Some people say, 'Oh, but when I got saved all my sins were forgiven.'

Look at Luke 11:4, where Jesus, some two years later, reiterates to His disciples how to pray.

> *'And forgive us our sins, For we ourselves also forgive everyone who is indebted to us. And lead us not into temptation.'*

There are a number of Greek words translated sin. The word 'sins' here, is the Greek word *hamartia*. It has the sense of **failing to reach the mark.**

God has set his standard for our lives. It has been spelt out as the Law. Jesus said the whole of the Law and the Prophets could be summed up in two commandments.

> *'And he answered and said, "You shall love the Lord your God with all your heart, and with all your soul, and with all your strength, and with all your mind; and your neighbor as yourself."'* (Luke 10:27)

When we fail to meet these standards God sets, we sin. Someone commented that if these are the two greatest commandments, then our greatest sin must be in not obeying them.

We too inwardly, set standards of how we feel others should treat us. When they fail to reach the mark we have set, we sense that there is a debt outstanding. According to Jesus, that debt needs to be dealt with.

1 John 1:9 says

> *'If we confess our sins, He is faithful and just to forgive us our sins and cleanse us from all unrighteousness.'*

There are big implications in these verses. If we don't forgive those who have offended (are indebted to) us, we still have sin in our heart, because the Lord has not forgiven us. If we have sin in our heart there is no cleansing and no righteousness.

In Luke 6 Jesus gave more practical teaching about handling hurt and conflict:

> *'But love your enemies, and do good, and lend, expecting nothing in return; and your reward will be great, and you will be sons of the Most High; for He Himself is kind to ungrateful and evil men. Be merciful, just as your Father is merciful. And do not judge and you will not be judged; and do not condemn, and you will not be condemned; pardon, and you will be pardoned.'*
> (Luke 6:20–38)

'Pardon' in the last verse is the Greek word *apoluo*. The New International Version translates it 'forgive'. It literally means **release**. We could therefore accurately render the last part of this verse; ***Release and you will be released.***

What is the context of that verse? It's to do with how you deal with those who hurt you. Forgiving them. But not only forgiving them, but releasing them.

Now read the next verse.

> *'Give, and it will be given to you; good measure, pressed down, shaken together, running over, they will pour into your lap. For by your standard of measure it will be measured to you in return.'*   (Luke 6:38)

I had always thought that this verse was to do with money. I have heard it quoted many times when offerings have been taken. (Actually, I believe the principle here can **also** apply to money.) But, the context of the verses preceding verse 38 is to do with forgiving and releasing.

So what do we give here? Surely forgiveness. What will be given to us? Forgiveness in

> ***'a good measure, pressed down, shaken together running over, they will pour into your lap. For by your standard of measure it will be measured to you in return.'***

17

Jesus is saying that if you want to be forgiven, you yourself must forgive. If you want to be released, you must release those who have hurt you and those who have mistreated you. If you give forgiveness, then God's forgiveness can be poured out on you.

Looking for the Breakthrough?

Many Christians live with unforgiveness in their heart and wonder why they can never get the breakthrough in God they are looking for. They wonder why they never move in power. They wonder why they rarely move in spiritual gifts. They've tried everything. They've listened to every tape from 'men of faith'. They've read every book for 'overcomers'. They've been to Bible Weeks and conferences, yet they still can't break through.

There is a good probability that there is still unforgiveness in their heart. Maybe you are one of those people. Right now you may be thinking that you don't have unforgiveness in your heart and that you are not owed in any way. If you are open to the Holy Spirit, why not pray now and let God show you as you read on.

Father, please will you show me if I have any areas of unforgiveness in my heart. I do not want to cover anything up. Please show me the things where I have claimed that they are 'under the blood', when in reality I have just swept them 'under the carpet'.

Chapter 4

The Unforgiving Servant

In Matthew 18, Jesus tells a parable to explain what He had just said to Peter about forgiveness. The parable is about settling accounts. Some of us, when we think about the people that hurt us, would like to settle accounts by doing to them what they did to us!

But first, let us read the conversation between Peter and Jesus in Matthew 18:21f.

> *'Then Peter came and said to Him, "Lord, how often shall my brother sin against me and I forgive him? Up to seven times?" Jesus said to him, "I do not say to you, up to seven times, but up to seventy times seven."'*

Jesus was not saying forgive the person 490 times, then on the 491st time clobber them! He was saying forgiveness has no limitations. Nor was He saying that when you think of a person who has wronged you, forgive them and if you think about it again, forgive them again for the same issue. Some Christians believe that constantly 'forgiving' someone for the same issue, will gradually take the pain away. It doesn't. Accounts have to be settled.

Look at 1 Corinthians 13:5

> *'(Love) ... does not act unbecomingly; it does not seek its own, is not provoked, does not take **into account** a wrong suffered.'*

19

The New English Bible says:

'Love keeps no score of wrongs.'

Some people imagine that God has an index card in heaven with their name on it, recording all the wrongs they do. When they sin and come to God, it seems that God digs out their index card. When they confess what they have done, God looks at the card and says, 'That's the 6th time you've done that this week. We had better put this one down as well.' He then 'lets them off' because they have confessed their sin.

God does not behave like that. He forgives us **and** releases us. If He were to pull out our imaginary card, He would say, 'Your card is clear. There's no record of any wrong here. You are sorry for your sin? I forgive you.' As a result, according to 1 John 1 verse 9, we would receive His righteousness and cleansing.

The parable that follows explains that if you forgive correctly a person who wrongs you, the next time it happens is like the first time it happened. You don't keep count. True forgiveness does not count how many wrongs have been done against us.

'For this reason the kingdom of heaven may be compared to a certain king who wished to settle accounts with his slaves. And when he had begun to settle them, there was brought to him one who owed him ten thousand talents. But since he did not have the means to repay, his lord commanded him to be sold, along with his wife and children and all that he had, and repayment to be made. The slave therefore falling down, prostrated himself before him, saying, "Have patience with me, and I will repay you everything." And the lord of that slave felt compassion and released him and forgave him the debt. But that slave went out and found one of his fellow slaves who owed him a hundred denarii; and he seized him and began to choke him, saying, "Pay back

what you owe." So his fellow slave fell down and began to entreat him, saying, "Have patience with me and I will repay you." He was unwilling however, but went and threw him in prison until he should pay back what was owed. So when his fellow slaves saw what had happened, they were deeply grieved and came and reported to their lord all that had happened. Then summoning him, his lord said to him, "You wicked slave, I forgave you all that debt because you entreated me. Should you not also have had mercy on your fellow slave, even as I had mercy on you?" And his lord, moved with anger, handed him over to the torturers until he should repay all that was owed him. So shall my heavenly Father also do to you, if each of you does not forgive his brother from your heart.'

(Matthew 18:23–35)

Notice some of the phrases:
- This parable is about **settling accounts**.
- One man **owed** the King, but couldn't pay.
- The King **felt compassion for him**.
- The King **released him**.
- The King **forgave him the debt**.
- The forgiven slave found a fellow slave and said **pay back what you owe**.
- When that slave asked for mercy **he was unwilling**.
- He threw his fellow slave **in prison until he paid back what was owed**.
- The King angered by what he heard said, **should you not also have had mercy on your fellow slave?**
- Because of the slave's lack of mercy and unforgiveness the King **handed him over to the torturers** until **he should repay all that was owed him**.

Verse 35 is quite mind boggling! Jesus said the Father would hand us over to the torturers, if we do not forgive our brother from our heart.

Think back to Deuteronomy 29. What did God say He

would do to the man who would walk with bitterness in his heart? He would single him out for adversity. Jesus is saying here, that if we don't forgive those who have offended us, don't think the Father will forgive us. We should forgive because we have been forgiven. Now let's make the parable contemporary and personal.

A bank manager desires to sort out those customers who are in arrears. You have a £100,000 mortgage and are 5 months behind in your payments, due to unemployment. The interest rate has just increased again. He invites you in for an interview to find out how you are going to pay the arrears. You really have no explanation. He then tells you the bad news that your house is to be repossessed, and your possessions sold until repayment is made. You break down in front of him, begging for more time.

This bank manager feels great compassion for you, knowing that you will never be able to pay, even if you get a job. He then says to you that he will personally clear the arrears and the outstanding mortgage in totality. In addition, he will clear your overdraft, credit cards, car loan and settle any hire purchase arrangements you have, leaving you debt free.

You leave his office a financially free man. Next day in the local pub you meet a man who owes you £50 for a repair job you did to his car 3 months ago. He's promised to pay you for ages, and still doesn't have the money. Angered, you take him to court to recover the debt.

One of his friends knows the manager of the bank and at lunch with him one day, tells him what happened. You get another call from the bank for another interview. This time he's the angry one. 'I said I would personally pay your debt, because you asked me for leniency. Why weren't you as lenient with your debtor as I was with you?' He then rescinds his previous decision. He sends you to court to have the repossession order carried out. You are bankrupted and left on the street penniless.

The analogy ends here. Bankrupts are not sent to prison and in modern prisons torture is not allowed!

I would like to point out five things.

1.   The King knew the servant couldn't pay back what he owed. Remember that this parable is teaching truth about our relationship with God and with others. We are the servant that owed the King ten thousand talents. There is no way that we could pay back to God what we owed him as a result of our sin. We call to God for mercy when we become a Christian. We ask Him to forgive us.

2.   The King felt compassion, released him and forgave him the debt. You see forgiveness was **not enough** for this man. It was not enough for the King to say him, 'I forgive you **for the fact that you owe me this money'**. Being given another 30 days to pay would not have helped. Ten thousand talents was probably far greater than the Gross National Product of Palestine in Jesus' day. If he had just 'forgiven' him, the man would have known there was still an outstanding debt. The King could still say at any time, 'You still owe me. Pay up.' For the man to experience **true forgiveness**, he needed releasing from the debt.

3.   The forgiven servant went out and met someone who owed him. When was he owed the 100 denarii? Before he was forgiven by the King or after he was forgiven and released by the King? From the text it seems that he was owed before the King had forgiven him.

Before going on to points four and five, what is the implication of the last point for us?

There are people who have offended us and things that have happened to us before we became Christians, that have wounded us making us feel owed. Just because we became a Christian, those things did not all get sorted out.

Some would like to believe that when they became a Christian everything became brand new. They quote verses like 2 Corinthians 5:17:

> *'Therefore if any man is in Christ, he is a new creature; the old things passed away; behold, new things have come.'*

But when we became a Christian, not **everything** we did became new. Our bank manager did not write off our mortgage at the good news of our salvation. Had we been through three divorces, we would not be instantly reconciled to all three wives! If you became a Christian while in prison, it did not mean that you could just walk free the next day. You still have to pay the penalty for your wrongdoing. There were many things that impacted our lives before we became a Christian, and those things can still affect us now.

Many people, particularly in evangelical churches, have been told that when they became a Christian, all their past was dealt with. Their past has no effect on them anymore. That kind of theology unfortunately lacks integrity. The terrorist who maims and murders one day, yet repents the next day is surely not released from the responsibility of his actions, is he? His salvation will not bring back to the bereaved families their loved ones. He must still face the consequences of his actions.

No, the new creation is to do with our **spirit**. We are body, soul and spirit. When we were born again, our spirit was renewed (Titus 3:5). When Jesus comes again we will get a new body (1 Corinthians 15:50–53). Meanwhile, God wants to sort out our personality – our thoughts, decisions and feelings.

Our spirit is regenerated by the working of the Holy Spirit. Our ability to know God intimately is changed by rebirth. Our conscience is cleansed and sharpened. We are given a new ability to worship the Creator as 'Daddy', not just as 'Almighty God, Maker of Heaven and Earth'. Our body certainly does not take on immortality at conversion! We must await the resurrection for that.

The truth is that there is still much that needs changing in us. The work yet to be done is primarily in our mind, will and emotions which have been damaged through sin and its effects. Right now God is still working in us to change us.

Consider these verses:

'For I am confident of this very thing, that He who began a good work in you will perfect it until the day of Christ Jesus.' (Philippians 1:6)

'So then, my beloved, just as you have always obeyed, not as in my presence only, but now much more in my absence, work out your salvation with fear and trembling;' (Philippians 2:12)

'I urge you therefore, brethren, by the mercies of God, to present your bodies a living and holy sacrifice, acceptable to God, which is your spiritual service of worship. And do not be conformed to this world, but be transformed by the renewing of your mind, that you may prove what the will of God is, that which is good and acceptable and perfect.' (Romans 12:1f)

'But we all, with unveiled face beholding as in a mirror the glory of the Lord, are being transformed into the same image from glory to glory, just as from the Lord, the Spirit.' (2 Corinthians 3:18)

However, the following verse teaches us that right now we are as righteous as God is.

'He made Him who knew no sin to be sin on our behalf, that we might become the righteousness of God in Him.' (2 Corinthians 5:21)

If, in Christ, I am the righteousness of God, what happens when I sin? Do I need to ask for forgiveness? Why do I need forgiveness if I'm righteous? Theologians can answer this question by explaining the difference between our 'standing' and our 'state' before God.

Our standing is what Christ has made us in eternal terms. Our state is how we are practically right now. If a beggar who lives on the street gets left a million pounds in a rich person's will, his standing is one of tremendous fortune.

His state may be that he currently lives in a cardboard box, has holes in his shoes and is broke. There are things that are going to have to change if he is to fully inherit his inheritance!

The same is true for us. Our spiritual inheritance is wonderful, but there is action that we need to take to appropriate it. The gospel we have believed has to be worked out practically, not just acknowledged theoretically. In Ephesians Paul writes:

> *'Therefore, laying aside falsehood, speak truth, each one of you, with his neighbor, for we are members of one another. Be angry, and yet do not sin; do not let the sun go down on your anger, and do not give the devil an opportunity. Let him who steals steal no longer; but rather let him labor, performing with his own hands what is good, in order that he may have something to share with him who has need. Let no unwholesome word proceed from your mouth, but only such a word as is good for edification according to the need of the moment, that it may give grace to those who hear. And do not grieve the Holy Spirit of God, by whom you were sealed for the day of redemption. Let all bitterness and wrath and anger and clamor and slander be put away from you, along with all malice. And be kind to one another, tender-hearted, forgiving each other, just as God in Christ also has forgiven you.'*
>
> (Ephesians 4:25–32)

This does not all happen automatically overnight! The Holy Spirit is continually working within us to change our character into the likeness of Jesus.

Now let's return to the parable in Matthew 18 –

4.   The servant did not have mercy on his fellow servant by forgiving and releasing him. It is inferred from the King's reply that he was expected to do so, **because** the King had forgiven and released him.

Are there not practical implications for us? This parable does not make sense if it only refers to that which lies in the future.

We need to wake up to the fact that there are debts outstanding in our lives from before we were Christians. Are we going to let people who 'owe' us stay locked up in a prison in our heart, bringing them out occasionally for a quick beating? Or are we going to open the account books of our emotions and start to settle accounts?

5.   The unforgiving servant was handed to the torturers to extract every last penny that he owed the King.

Jesus promises that the Father will do the same to us if we do not forgive from our heart.

Chapter 5

The Soil of Insecurity

Let's look again at the picture.

```
┌─────────────────────────────────────────┐
│                          Fruit           │
│     Seed                                  │
│                                           │
│  ≈≈≈≈≈≈≈≈≈≈≈≈≈≈≈≈≈≈≈≈≈≈≈≈≈≈≈≈≈≈≈≈≈≈       │
│     Soil                                  │
│                          Root             │
│                                           │
└─────────────────────────────────────────┘
```

When God first showed me this picture, He told me to draw it for people when I was helping them to forgive others, so that they could see the process involved.

When we have a truly secure relationship with somebody, we can usually say anything without causing or receiving offence from them. For example, I have a good friend called Jeremy, and also a nose shaped like a wedge. Jeremy says to me, 'Joff, if you had a nose like that on the back of your head, you could get a job as a pickaxe!'

Now, because I know Jeremy – that he loves me and is for me – I do not take offence. I can enjoy the joke telling him that a monkey tried to pick my nose the other day, thinking it was a banana.

But what if a total stranger walking on the beach with his wife were to see me lying on my back sunbathing and say to her in my hearing, 'Stack me love. That bloke's nostrils look like the entrance to Eurotunnel!' That could be a totally different matter! I could be very hurt. (In fact, with four children and friends like Jeremy, I am very secure about my physical appearance!)

There are times when friends who are close to me need to come and tell me the truth about myself, that they know will hurt. The Bible calls it *'speaking the truth in love'* (Ephesians 4:15). Their words cut me, not to expose me and leave me emotionally bleeding, but so that that which needs to change in me can be dealt with.

These are the *'faithful'* wounds of Proverbs 27:5 which come to bring healing to my life. There is no 'offence' in their words. They have not taken from me anything which did not need to go. I do not feel owed by them. I'm grateful that they love me enough to come and tell me my faults.

Someone once said, 'Love without truth is sentimentality and truth without love is brutality.' Someone else once said that before you take your ten ton truck of 'truth' to another person, you had better make sure there is more than a matchstick bridge of relationship and security between you. If you don't, great damage and offence can be caused.

In the parable of the Sower in Mark 4, Jesus mentions different kinds of soil that the word of God is sown in. It was the soil type that determined the growth. For a seed to take root effectively, there had to be good soil. The soil is of course referring to the hearts of the listeners.

The fundamental reason we have been hurt in the past, and are liable to get hurt in the future is this – we have the soil of insecurity in our heart.

```
┌─────────────────────────────────────────────┐
│                          Fruit                │
│                                               │
│    Seed                                       │
│                                               │
│   ≈≈≈≈≈≈≈≈≈≈≈≈≈≈≈≈≈≈≈≈≈≈≈≈≈≈≈≈≈≈≈≈≈≈≈         │
│   Soil of                                     │
│   Insecurity              Root                │
│                                               │
└─────────────────────────────────────────────┘
```

Divine Purpose

God's intention is that the soil of our heart is to be tended and nurtured primarily by our father and mother in the early years of our development. The home should be a place of love, appreciation, acceptance and encouragement. As our personality (mind, will and emotions) develops, the correct balance of love and discipline produces security within us.

If good seed, consisting not only of actions, but words of love, affirmation and encouragement are sown, then, in time, there will be the fruit of that in our lives. The good seed will produce a harvest of those positive attributes that we can give to others. The fruit of the Spirit (Galatians 5) will flourish in abundance. If we have the soil of security within us, when seeds of offence or hurt come, we can deal with them constructively.

But if the soil in our hearts is the soil of insecurity resulting from a less than perfect (dysfunctional) family background, two things happen.

First, any good seed that is sown finds difficulty in taking root. The soil may be shallow, full of stones and rocks. It may have thorns and thistles growing that choke out the good seed.

Secondly, the soil of insecurity provides a fertile ground

31

for the seeds of hurts and disappointments to take root quickly.

I have yet to meet anyone that has come from a perfect family background! Sociologists tell us that most of our families were dysfunctional to some extent. The implication is that we all have areas of insecurity within us. None of us are as secure as we think we are!

The problem is that we have got used to rationalising the hurts that come our way. As a result, we don't ever deal with the emotional damage properly.

Now let's look at the seed.

Chapter 6

The Seed of Offence

A root usually starts as a seed that has been planted. I want to call the things that hurt us the Seed of Offence. Let's look at the picture again.

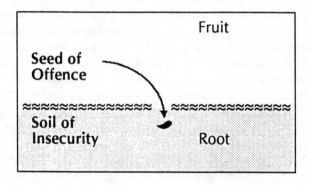

There are seeds of offence that get sown into the insecure soil of our lives producing a harvest after their own kind. The seeds germinate and produce a root as well as fruit.

There are four basic ways that those seeds of offence get sown into us.

1. What others said to us

Some people grow up constantly being told, 'You're useless' 'You're no good', 'You'll never amount to anything',

'You're just like your father ... a loser', 'You're a failure'. Some people are told 'You're ugly', 'You're fat', 'Rabbit ears', 'You smell', 'You've got fleas'.

To cope with the indignities, we're reminded to sing the little rhyme:

> Sticks and stones may break my bones
> But names will never hurt me.

That rhyme is a lie from the pit of hell! As a kid I said it and tried to believe it, but the names still hurt! I would have preferred a few sticks and stones! I knew cuts and bruises on my legs got better. The feelings that went with being called names never seemed to.

You see, names hurt. Names wound. Always being reminded of our weaknesses and failings hurt us. Do you know what happens when someone calls us stupid, useless, failure? We are being robbed! We are being robbed of self-worth. We are being robbed of dignity. We are being robbed of a sense of value. How do I know that? Because we are made to feel less as a result of what has been said. Suddenly there is a debt there. Suddenly we feel owed.

If we get enough negative things said to us, we can end up losing all self-respect. Not only do we hate those who have offended us, but we end up hating ourselves. We look in the mirror and say the same things we have heard. We speak to ourselves and say 'You're ugly ... I hate you!'

I have counselled both teens and adults who told me that they have sat in front of a mirror speaking hate and curses to themselves.

2. What others did not say to you

Think of all the encouragement you needed as a kid, but didn't get. As I said earlier, God's plan for mothers and fathers is to encourage their children, to build them up, to bless them, to speak good things into them. But how many times did we miss hearing, 'Son I think you're great ... I really love you'. 'Darling, it really doesn't matter that you failed your Maths exam. I still think you're wonderful!'

Some of us missed that kind of unconditional love and acceptance. We were brought up to understand that love is performance based. If we did well we felt accepted. If we didn't make the grade, we were rejected.

What was worse, was if we thought we had done well and deserved praise, and it didn't come. What wasn't said to us, hurt as much as the negative things that had been spoken to us. It hurt deep down on the inside. It hurt when someone did as well as us and was congratulated, yet no one said anything to us. As a result we feel robbed. We feel owed those words of encouragement that never came. We feel owed the words of approval that never came.

The scripture records two occasions when God rolled back the clouds of heaven and spoke of His Son. The first was at His baptism, when He spoke to Jesus personally.

> *'and the Holy Spirit descended upon Him in bodily form like a dove. And a voice came from heaven, "You are my Son, the Beloved; with you I am well pleased."'*
> (Luke 3:22 NIV)

It seems that even Jesus needed to hear words of approval from His Father. God was, in effect saying, 'I love you Son, I think you're great.' If Jesus needed to hear the words, how much more should we?

The second occasion was at Jesus' transfiguration. Here, He spoke to those who were with Jesus.

> *'While He was still speaking, suddenly a bright cloud overshadowed them, and from the cloud a voice said, "This is my Son, the Beloved; with Him I am well pleased; listen to Him!"'* (Matthew 17:5 NIV)

Fathers should not only give personal approval and affirmation to their sons. They should also be prepared to speak well of their sons when others are around. How many can think back to the days when we were put down in front of others by those who should be building us up. We feel robbed. We feel owed.

Many dozens of people I have spoken to said the same thing:

> 'I suppose my dad told me he loved me, but I don't ever remember it.'

> 'I suppose my mum must have said she loved me loads of times, but I just can't recall one.'

There's an ache in their heart. There's a void in their heart where they feel owed those words of love and acceptance.

3. What others did to us

Today the newspapers and TV documentaries give us constant reminders that we live in a society permeated by abuse. Domestic and marital violence, sexual and child abuse are all on the increase. In reality, these increases may only be apparent as people are becoming more honest about what is actually going on. 95% of all sexual abusers of children are men. Many surveys show that most abusers were abused themselves.

Recently there have been reports on young people who have committed suicide due to constant bullying at school. Any kind of physical abuse leaves you feeling owed, leaves you feeling robbed.

Some people who read this book will have been sexually abused. For some, the only way to deal with the pain and anguish caused by the abuse, is to bury the issue. Pretend it didn't happen. But all that really happens is that a lid gets put on the 'sewer' within.

When a person is abused sexually, they have been robbed. Ask any single woman who has never had sex and then been raped. She's had her virginity ripped from her. She's owed.

'I know my father said he would never do it again, but he couldn't help it. He said himself that it's what his father did to him.' A woman who was sexually abused by her father may make excuses that satisfy her mind, but they don't reduce the pain within.

If the woman who experienced that trauma becomes a Christian, everything does not necessarily become wonderful now. There can still be hurt.

My mother was recently visiting my father who was in a London hospital for a minor operation. She had travelled on the train and was walking the last few yards to the hospital. Suddenly a young man ripped her handbag off her arm and dashed away into the crowd of people. She was thrown to the floor, powerless to do anything. Thankfully she was not physically hurt other than a few bruises. Her handbag contained money, credit cards and all the other usual paraphernalia ladies carry! The Police told her there was little or no hope of recovering her bag, even though the thief was probably only interested in her cash.

It's obvious she felt owed. But the situation is more subtle than that. She was robbed of time; contacting the Police, ringing round to cancel credit cards, writing to confirm details. She was robbed of her sense of security and peace ... this happened in broad daylight on a busy street. The thief would have been able to get her address from the contents of the bag and maybe he would plan to burgle her house. Could she make him repay what he owed?

But it's not just major traumas that can leave you feeling owed. What about the careless driver who scraped the paint off your car door in the car park and just left a slip of paper on your windscreen saying, 'Sorry pal!' Doesn't he owe you? How are you going to make him pay?

What about the time when a careless child ran past you in the playground and ripped your new school dress. You were the one who got blamed by your parents despite your protests. You can still feel owed years later ... even if you've become a Christian.

4. What people didn't do

This is probably the biggest one of the four. Unfulfilled expectations. Disappointments.

'If you pass your exams, then daddy will buy you that mountain bike you've seen in the shop in town.'

Expectation in you rises sky high. You know that if you put the extra effort in you can pass. The results come through and you get straight A's. But there's been a shake up at your father's firm and he loses his job. There is no redundancy pay. Dad is very apologetic. 'Son, I'm sorry, but we don't have the money to get you the bike.' In your mind you rationalise the situation. 'We've got no money, we can't afford a bike.' But your emotions are not rational. They tell you 'I'm owed a bike. He promised me a bike.'

Years later you cannot understand why you get angry at small injustices in your life. The truth is that the feelings of injustice go right back to when you were owed the bike by your father. In fact, if you go back to the issue in your mind, you can still feel how you felt twenty years ago. The account is still outstanding in your emotions. You still feel owed. There's a debt that needs dealing with.

Look at Proverbs 13:12

> *'Hope deferred makes the heart sick, but desire fulfilled is a tree of life.'*

It was Hannibal Smith from the TV series *The A Team* who said 'I love it when a plan comes together!' We are all like that. Isn't it wonderful when your plans come together? It could be a romantic weekend away with your wife, that you've been keeping secret for months. Or a special holiday abroad for the first time. Maybe the house you really wanted but that had been sold, is back on the market at £5000 less than you were prepared to pay. Desire fulfilled is a tree of life. When things go well, we want to go YESSS! like the little boy in the film *Home Alone*!

But what about a plan when it hasn't worked out; when

it's gone wrong? It makes the heart sick. The word sick means afflicted, ill, weak, faint and wounded.

Many of us have had promises made to us that have been broken. The broken promises that hurt the most are by authority figures in our lives. Primarily this means our parents. But it also includes teachers and especially church leaders. Church leaders unwittingly wound many of their flock by making promises they do not keep, or cannot keep. They may promise to encourage, approve and affirm us, but rarely are they able to give us the time or input we feel we need.

Why do we get hurt by this? It is because we believe that what those authority figures say must be the truth. Not only that, they seem to have the power to fulfil what they have said. Again, it is so easy to rationalise it all and make excuses. 'Well it's not their fault, circumstances have changed.' But on the inside, at what we call gut level, it hurts.

God's plan is to heal the hurts from the past. Part of His method is forgiving and releasing. When Jesus began His ministry He spelled out His commission this way:

> *'The Spirit of the Lord is upon Me, because He anointed Me to preach the gospel to the poor. He has sent Me to proclaim release to the captives, and recovery of sight to the blind, to set free those who are downtrodden, to proclaim the favorable year of the Lord.'*
>
> (Luke 4:18f)

The Living Bible says:

> *'...he has sent me to heal the brokenhearted and to announce that captives shall be released and the blind shall see, that the downtrodden shall be freed from their oppressors...'*

Part of this commission is to set free the downtrodden, to bind the brokenhearted. Does this mean the physical healing of the organ that pumps blood round our body? No. It's to do with healing damaged emotions. If hope deferred makes the heart sick, then Jesus is the person to come to for healing!

Why was the proclamation of the favourable year of the Lord good news to the poor? The favourable year of the Lord was the Year of Jubilee, which came round every 50 years. You can read about it in Leviticus 25. It was the year of cancelled debt. Whatever you owed another person was cancelled in that year. This meant that in every person's lifetime, there was the possibility of being free from debt.

Jesus was talking here about debt cancellation. This was primarily in the sense of sins; falling short of God's standards. The good news is that you can have your debt against God wiped out. You can be forgiven for your sin.

Consider some more reasons for there being outstanding debts in your life:

- physical illness or disease either personal or in a parent, robs us of health and happiness
- physical or mental handicap
- trauma, for example
  - war
  - imprisonment
  - sudden death of a parent or close relation
  - divorce
- substance abuse, for example
  - an alcoholic or drug dependent parent
- religious bigotry or piety, for example
  - children brought up in strict religious order, robbed of their personality
- adoption and fostering
  - Did you get a good deal?
- family ambition and control
  - Were you sacrificed on the altar of your father's ambition?
    For example, did you have no friends because you went to 12 different schools in 14 years because of your father's promotion in his job? Children of ministers and church leaders are also hurt because of this.

All these can cause major hurt and disruption in the formative years of a person's life.

In our school and college years, subtle family control can result in frustration, anger and resentment in later life. Because we had to become something someone else wanted us to be, we can feel robbed of our own personality.

For example, did you have to carry your parent's Christian name?

'Hi! My name is John Dunkin. This is my son, John Dunkin Junior and his little boy will be John Dunkin III.'

Did you have to follow in the footsteps of a parent's career?

'Father, grandfather and great grandfather before him all went to the same college at Cambridge, so must you.'

'This family's military history is unique, son. **We** (you) must keep the family name in the Regiment.'

'We have a long nursing tradition in this family, dear. You wouldn't want to break it would you?'

'Every branch of this family has had someone enter the Anglican ministry. Now you wouldn't want to spoil things by becoming a non-conformist, would you?'

We often feel that there is no need to forgive that which is 'understandable' human frailty or shortcoming. The real question is though, **do we 'feel' owed?** Often our real feelings have been rationalised in order to cope. Christian teaching on 'ruling' our thoughts and emotions has meant that we **control** the pain and disappointment of the past rather than **confront** it. Sadly, much 'ruling' is fooling!

Having read the above list, you may now need to re-read this chapter, but without making excuses for those who 'owe' you. Ask God to let you make contact with any feelings you have buried. You may find you have some debt cancelling to do!

Maybe you could pray this:

> Heavenly Father, You know that I have tried to for-
> give. I have to admit that I still feel owed by some. I
> have tried to bury the hurt, but it is still there. Please
> show me everywhere I have forgiven at a mind level,
> but not from the heart.

If you are not yet a Christian, and would like to be, go to
Appendix A at the back of this book. When you know that
you yourself have been forgiven and released by God, you
will be able to truly forgive and release others.

Chapter 7

The Root of Bitterness

If no action is taken to remove the Seed of Offence, it quickly germinates. Two things happen. A root goes down and a shoot goes up.

Let us look at how the picture is developing.

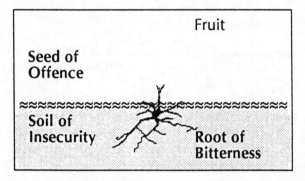

When you get hurt on the inside by any of the four things mentioned in the last chapter, the effect is first under the surface. You can keep a smile on your face, 'It's OK Dad, don't worry about the bike.' But on the inside the reaction may be, 'You liar! . . . I'll kill you one day.'

Can reactions be that extreme? I have talked to people who would have liked to murder their father because of what he did. That is how hurt they were on the inside. That kind of attitude spreads like cancer on the inside. It becomes a root of bitterness within.

> '*Wash your heart from evil, O Jerusalem, that you may be saved. **How long will your wicked thoughts lodge within you?** For a voice declares from Dan, And proclaims wickedness from Mount Ephraim. "Report it to the nations, now! Proclaim over Jerusalem, Besiegers come from a far country, and lift their voices against the cities of Judah. Like watchmen of a field they are against her round about, Because she has rebelled against Me," declares the Lord. "Your ways and your deeds Have brought these things to you. This is your evil. **How bitter! How it has touched your heart!"** My soul, my soul! I am in anguish! Oh, my heart! My heart is pounding in me; I cannot be silent, Because you have heard, O my soul, The sound of the trumpet, The alarm of war.*' (Jeremiah 4:14–19)

In these verses we can see the effect of sin on the emotions. Bitterness is linked with agony in the heart.

> '*But if you have **bitter jealousy and selfish ambition in your heart**, do not be arrogant and so lie against the truth. This wisdom is not that which comes down from above, but is earthly, natural, demonic. **For where jealousy and selfish ambition exist, there is disorder and every evil thing.**'* (James 3:14–16)

If there is a root of bitterness in a person's life, sooner or later it will surface.

The root of bitterness:

1 is poison. It eats away at you on the inside.
2 causes anguish and pain in the heart.
3 is associated with jealousy and selfish ambition, – 'I'll show them'.
4 provides an entrance for demonic activity.
   When it springs up (becoming external), it
5 causes trouble
6 defiles many – to defile means to contaminate or to pollute

Bitterness works on the inside in two ways:

1. What you feel

When somebody hurts you, other than physically, the first place it gets you is not in the mind but in the 'guts'. It hurts in the pit of the stomach. Jesus had perfectly balanced emotions. However, He was not unfeeling when He saw the plight of others.

> *'And behold, two blind men sitting by the road, hearing that Jesus was passing by, cried out, saying, "Lord, have mercy on us, Son of David!" And the multitude sternly told them to be quiet; but they cried out all the more, saying, "Lord, have mercy on us, Son of David!" And Jesus stopped and called them, and said, "What do you want Me to do for you?" They said to Him, "Lord, we want our eyes to be opened." And* **moved with compassion**, *Jesus touched their eyes; and immediately they regained their sight and followed Him.'* (Matthew 20: 30–34)

> *'I* **feel compassion** *for the multitude because they have remained with Me now three days, and have nothing to eat;'* (Mark 8:2)

The Greek word for compassion is almost unpronounceable unless you are Greek or a Greek scholar. It is *splagchnizomai*, pronounced splangkh-nid'-zom-ahee. It means:

to have the bowels yearn; to be moved in the inward parts; to be filled with tenderness.

In Eastern culture the bowels were understood to be the seat of the emotions. In today's vernacular we would say that when Jesus heard the blind men's plea for help, it got Him in the guts.

Remember Matthew 18? What was said of the slave's Lord when he saw he could not pay? **He was moved with compassion**. It's the same Greek word.

When we get hurt, when the seed of offence is sown, it gets us in the guts. If we do not deal with it, the root goes down and the shoot springs up and ultimately bears the fruit of resentment. We can try to bury the issue and years later we will suddenly hear a name that triggers off in us a torrent of hurt feelings. We wonder where it all came from. The truth is, it came from the 'sewer of hurt feelings' within. We feel owed, we feel hurt, we feel bitter.

Bitterness can be experienced in varying degrees. Something can be so bitter to the taste that your tongue wants to crawl down your throat. Or bitterness can just be a bad taste left in the mouth. In fact when something unpleasant happens to us, we might even use the expression that 'It left a bitter taste in my mouth'. Sadly, experiences that we have had both before and after conversion have left a bad taste in our mouth.

Here are some of the characteristic emotions that go with these experiences.

A sense of injustice

'It's not fair.' That's one of the biggest emotions to cope with when we have been hurt. In fact, it is one of the easiest ways to know whether we are really hurting on the inside or not. If we do not feel we can change our circumstances; if we feel we are out of control, then we sense injustice. If we do not overcome it, then we feel frustrated.

Frustration

Frustration comes as a result of some hope, some aspiration, some action we take being thwarted. It also comes as a result of someone else thwarting our plans and hopes. If a root of bitterness is already at work in us, then the out-working of that frustration is anger. Good sense is overruled by negative emotion.

For example; we get to the station in plenty of time to

catch our train, which will get us to the airport with just enough time to catch our plane. At the time the train should leave it stays stationary at the platform. We look at our watch. Five minutes pass and we begin to get irritated and fidgety. Our worst suspicions about British Rail are being realised.

After ten minutes a guard comes through the carriage asking everyone to leave this train and go to one on platform 15 that is due to leave in two minutes. Our temperature is rising fast. It will take at least a minute to get off the train and find a luggage trolley. We finally blow up at the guard, 'Why can't you lot ever get it right?!'

The guard then explains that there has been a major derailment a mile further up the track, and it is thought that 15 people may be dead as a result. All trains are having to be diverted. We respond with a grunt.

We have a choice to make at this point. Do we let frustration become anger at how inconvenienced we have been? Do we start to sizzle like the proverbial pressure cooker? Or do we realise that the source of our inconvenience, the source of our frustrated plans is a mass of tangled metal and bodies where lives have been shattered and torn apart?

If there is no root of bitterness within, we feel ashamed that we had so quickly pre-judged circumstances that we knew nothing about. We apologise to the guard and making our exit for the alternative train, we pray for the wounded and dying and their families. Patience is the opposite to frustration. It is a fruit of the Holy Spirit that enables us to persevere and endure.

If there is a root of bitterness within, our response could be quite different. We feel justified in our criticism of British Rail. After all, it was probably their fault the derailment happened. Not only that, if we miss that plane, they are going to pay for it. They will have to pay for another ticket, pay for our hotel accommodation, pay for extra meals we will have to buy. We intend to **make them pay** for what they owe us.

Anger

The injustice does not have to have been suffered person-ally. One lady my wife and I were counselling had a con-tinual problem with anger. We asked about her childhood and found that her parents adopted a boy when she was small. The father always treated the boy differently to the rest of the family. He was always more harsh and demand-ing on the boy than on the other children.

She had tried to protect him, taking on herself all the unfairness with which he was treated. Years later, her adopted brother had become a homosexual. As we were talking she suddenly saw that she felt great anger and resentment towards her father for the way he treated her adopted brother.

Until then, she had not realised the source of her anger. When she got angry either with her children or husband, it always seemed to be totally out of proportion to the preced-ing circumstances. When she confronted the hurt within, and forgave and released her father, great healing came into her life.

Anger is a natural consequence of frustration. Trying to slacken a wheel nut on a car, the wheel brace slips off resulting in gashed knuckles on the gravel in the gutter. The motorist, in frustration, throws the wheelbrace at the ground where it bounces back, hitting his shin with great force.

Who was to blame for this incident? Who is the motorist really angry at? The wheelbrace? The car? The mechanic who over-tightened the nut or himself, for not taking more care? Anger is always an expression of emotion towards people, not towards things. More often than not, it is the venting of the hurts and injustices experienced in a person's past, whether recent or not.

Like a volcano, anger can be waiting to explode on some poor unsuspecting person. Somebody can come along and say something quite innocently, but the response is an eruption of hurt feelings within. It is just like someone came along and pricked a boil and all the pus splattered out over anyone nearby. Hebrews 12:15 says the root of bitterness **springs up**. It is almost as if one minute it is not there and the next it is.

That kind of person ends up being harsh and judgmental like the elder brother in the parable of the lost son. They become a perfectionist, demanding of themselves and others standards that cannot be met.

What is the answer? The answer is not to put another plaster on the boil. The answer is to deal with the boil, to drain the poison and infection out, to disinfect the wound, and enable it to be healed.

Hatred

Anger, if not handled correctly, can easily become hatred.

'I hate my father for what he did. Even though he's dead, I hate him.'

I have heard people say that. Their parents have been dead and buried long ago, but they still hate them. They still feel owed. Extreme anger becomes hatred. It becomes hatred of those who have offended or hurt them. They only have to think of the name of the person and their countenance changes. They can feel the venom within. But if the venom within is not removed, it will eat away and poison every part of that person's being. Like cancer, it will destroy them.

Some people shift their anger on to themselves. Hatred also gets turned on themselves. They will scratch, bite and inflict pain on themselves. They will literally bang their head against a wall until it is bruised and bleeding. Why? Because **it's** unfair.

Anger and hatred can be expressed verbally and physically. I call this the Fruit of Resentment. It is the external manifestation of that which is within.

Violence is an expression of a sense of injustice felt deep within. The riots we have seen flaring up on council estates are as a result of years of tension built up on the inside of the residents, particularly young people. For many it is the frustration at the injustice of being jobless. They feel owed by the firm that made them redundant; owed by the company that would not give them a job and owed by the government for seemingly doing nothing. Eventually the hurt, the anger and the hatred gets taken out on people and property.

If anger and hatred do not get expressed, they get suppressed; pushed down on the inside until they apparently disappear. But the result is often depression. Often, someone who is depressed either has unforgiveness in their life as a result of some injustice done, or they are afflicted by a demon.

Demons can easily gain access to people through their unforgiveness. Unforgiveness is a rejection of Jesus' sacrifice on the Cross.

God's perspective on emotion

Anger is an emotion that is a part of every normal human being.

> *'Be angry, and yet do not sin; do not let the sun go down on your anger, and do not give the devil an opportunity.'* (Ephesians 4:26–27)

This scripture says that it is possible to be angry and not sin. The way you can be angry and not sin is to forgive and release the person that made you angry. It is not something that should be left for a few days, a few months, or a few years. 'Do not let the sun go down' means do it today, do it now.

There are many instances in the Bible where God is angry.

> *'Now the Lord was angry with Solomon because his heart was turned away from the Lord, the God of Israel, who had appeared to him twice.'* (1 Kings 11:9)

Even Jesus got angry. Having entered a synagogue, He came across a man with a withered hand. He then asked the Pharisees if it was right to heal on the Sabbath.

'And after looking around at them with anger, grieved at their hardness of heart, He said to the man, "Stretch out your hand." And he stretched it out, and his hand was restored.' (Mark 3:5)

But the Bible also tells us:

'For His anger is but for a moment, His favor is for a lifetime; Weeping may last for the night, But a shout of joy comes in the morning.' (Psalm 30:5)

and

'But Thou, O Lord, art a God merciful and gracious, Slow to anger and abundant in lovingkindness and truth.' (Psalm 86:15)

God can also hate:

'For I, the Lord, love justice, I hate robbery in the burnt offering...' (Isaiah 61:8)

Because of the unfaithfulness of Israel, He said:

'I hate, I reject your festivals, Nor do I delight in your solemn assemblies. But let justice roll down like waters and righteousness like an ever-flowing stream.'
(Amos 5:21, 24)

Psalm 45:7 speaks prophetically of the Lord Jesus:

'Thou hast loved righteousness, and hated wickedness; Therefore God, Thy God, has anointed Thee with the oil of joy above Thy fellows.' (Psalm 45:7)

So we see that it is possible to be angry and to hate without sin, provided that the subjects of our anger and hate are the same as God's.

51

Ephesians 4:27 in The Living Bible says,

> *'for when you are angry, you give a mighty foothold to the devil.'*

Footholds quickly become strongholds. What was once a 'tendency' to anger becomes an almost uncontrollable reflex. When anger becomes this deep-seated, demons may well gain access.

Bitterness not only expresses itself internally in our feelings, but also in:

2. What you think

> *'"Wash your heart from evil, O Jerusalem, that you may be saved. How long will your **wicked** thoughts lodge within you?*
>
> *"Your ways and your deeds Have brought these things to you. This is your evil. How bitter! How it has touched your heart!" My soul, my soul! I am in anguish! Oh, my heart! My heart is pounding in me; I cannot be silent, Because you have heard, O my soul, The sound of the trumpet, The alarm of war.'*
>
> (Jeremiah 4:14–19)

Despite denial, the bitterness affects our thinking. It twists and distorts our perception of life. As a result we start to form false assumptions about life. We develop thought patterns which form our beliefs. If we were told we were useless, despite many achievements in our lives, we still view ourselves as failures. We can be our own worst enemy sometimes, reinforcing the negatives. My wife Elaine's own testimony may help to illustrate this last point.

> 'From my early teens I can remember feeling "not good enough". Even though my family always approved of my achievements and encouraged me, I "knew" that as a person I was useless.

When I met Joff and married him, I could not believe that he could possibly love me ... I was ugly, useless and unlovable and didn't deserve loving. The first few years of our marriage were very difficult for Joff because I just couldn't receive his love. He showed me from the Bible that God loved me and that I had to love myself. I knew that God's word was true and chose to believe it. Through many ups and downs and much perseverance I came to a place where I ruled my thinking and was able to receive Joff's love and God's.

Even so, underneath I "knew" I was still no good. I tried to be what I thought I should be and what everyone else thought I should be. But when tough issues arose or I failed in some way, I dropped back into my old way of thinking "Well you're useless anyway. What did you expect?"

Not so long back God started to deal with me showing me just how insecure I really was. Some of the emotions that started to surface were irritation (at the smallest things), anger, jealousy, intolerance, resentment and the fact that I had been trying to manipulate circumstances for years.

I knew I could not carry on with this conflict and asked some friends to pray for me. They prayed and broke a number of strongholds in my thinking. The next day I felt somewhat better, but knew God was bringing more grot to the surface. Two days later, desperate to be set free, my friends prayed for me again. This time the Holy Spirit came on me powerfully and I began to shake, feeling a great pressure inside me wanting to break out. Sarah had a picture of the story of the Ugly Duckling, and shared that I was trying to be an ugly duckling, when really I was a swan.

Like a bolt of lightning revelation came to me. I had wasted years trying to conform to an image of myself that God had not intended. Even other people had tried to squeeze me into "their" mould not mine. I laughed. I cried. I couldn't take it in. As people and experiences passed before my eyes, I could see it all. I was not a duck, I **am** a swan!

I prayed, forgiving and releasing the people who had tried to mould me into a duck. What release came to me that Monday evening! I realised that I was always disappointed with myself, thinking I was an ugly duckling when in fact **all the time** I was a swan. They cast out a religious spirit and broke the power of the wrong thinking.

After everyone had gone, I went upstairs, looked in the mirror and for the first time in my life, looked myself straight in the eye and said, "You're beautiful" and **believed** it!

What joy there now is in being me. I love myself and actually believe that other people love me and like me. It's fantastic! All the arguments have gone. The resentment, anger and jealousy have all gone. What a relief it is to stop trying to be something God never wanted me to be. I'm not an ugly duckling – I'm a swan!'

Elaine's experience is probably similar to hundreds of other people's. Our distorted thinking affects everything. For example, if our father was a harsh disciplinarian, we form the view that God, our heavenly Father is the same.

We can also react in an equal and opposite way. If we were harshly disciplined as a child, we can make the decision that we will **never** do that with our children. When children eventually do come, we wonder why they are so insecure. It's because we have set no limits for them. There are no consequences for their wrongdoing.

What makes matters worse is when you do decide to discipline them. This results in confusion for them. The child is left not knowing where they are with you. Their perception is that the goalposts keep getting moved. Instead of building security in the child, you reinforce insecurity . . . fertile ground for the seed of offence and all we have touched on so far.

Someone once said 'Misuse of something that is good is not a reason for non-use. The answer is correct use.' Sadly the bitterness in our heart from our own experience distorts our thinking.

Chapter 8

The Fruit of Resentment

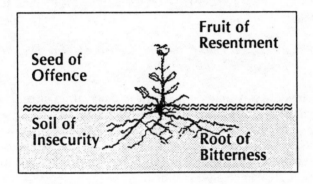

If those who have offended us have not been forgiven and released, then at some point, the root of bitterness surfaces in the fruit of resentment.

In 1992 Mount Etna on Sicily was threatening to erupt. The pressure build-up was so great that the lava burst out the side of the volcano, flowing down the side threatening to engulf a whole town. Drastic measures were needed to protect the town and its villagers. Many people, even Christians, are like volcanoes waiting to erupt. There is the pain and heartache of their past bubbling away on the inside.

Have you ever met 'prickly' people; quick-tempered, touchy people? They are the kind of people that you don't get too close to. They are similar to someone who has boils. Just dare to touch them! Anyone who has ever had a boil knows what I mean. If someone brushes past your boil, it's painful. Those people are usually like that because they are suppressing emotional pain inside themselves. Yet they try to put on a good face and say the right things. They were told as a child 'Keep a stiff upper lip'; 'Big boys don't cry'. All the emotion that needed to be expressed at the time just got buried.

The British 'stiff upper lip' is a con. It has deluded us into thinking we are in control. After all, what on earth would happen if all those emotions came out? If you have said those words inwardly, you need to let God heal the hurts. He's the one who sent His Son to heal the brokenhearted.

Psalm 34:18 says

> *'The Lord is near to the brokenhearted, and saves those who are crushed in spirit.'*

The only way many know how to deal with pain and hurt from the past is to treat it like the basement of a house with rats. You lock the door to the basement, and throw away the key. But God does not want us to have a basement of unresolved issues within us. He wants to get the 'rats' out, so that He can cleanse and heal.

When Hezekiah became King, he set his heart to make a covenant with God. As part of his reforms, he gave instructions to the Levites concerning the temple.

> *'Then he said to them, "Listen to me, O Levites. Consecrate yourselves now, and consecrate the house of the LORD, the God of your fathers, and carry the uncleanness out from the holy place." So the priests went in to the inner part of the house of the LORD to cleanse it, and every unclean thing which they found in the temple of the LORD they brought out to the court of the house of the LORD. Then the Levites received it to carry out to the Kidron valley.'* (2 Chronicles 29:5, 16)

It took 14 men 16 days to complete the cleansing. What

followed can only be described as a revival. Sacrifices were made, worship began again, the Passover was celebrated and in 2 Chronicles 30:20 it says,

> *'So the* LORD *heard Hezekiah, and healed the people.'*

The people were so blessed they decided to celebrate the feast again for another 7 days!

The New Testament, speaking of Israel as a picture of the Church says that:

> *'Now these things happened to them as an example, and they were written for our instruction, upon whom the ends of the ages have come.'*   (1 Corinthians 10:11)

1 Corinthians 6:19 says:

> *'... do you not know that your body is a temple of the Holy Spirit who is in you, whom you have from God, and that you are not your own?'*

God is far more interested in what we are like on the inside than what we are like on the outside. He is not too bothered whether we wear a flowery shirt or a plain shirt on a Sunday. Wearing jeans and jumper or a three-piece suit doesn't really matter. What He is really interested in is our heart.

We, as individuals, are a temple of God. Is there that which is 'unclean' in our inner part? No amount of excuses or denial makes the hurt go away. No amount of busyness ... even for God ... can deal with it. If there is that which is unclean, there is a need to go into the inner part and get the rubbish out.

If the root of bitterness is not dealt with, it will produce the fruit of resentment in our lives. That resentment comes out in two ways.

1. What you say

My experience has convinced me that someone who is always talking negatively has a root of bitterness in their life. This is as a result of unforgiveness somewhere in their past.

> '...*for the mouth speaks out of that which fills the heart.*'
> (Matthew 12:34)

This kind of person is a habitual fault finder! They find it so much easier to criticise others, than find something good to say. Nothing ever seems to be right. The weather is never right. The government (whichever is in power) is never right. Other drivers on the road are wrong. In extremes it comes out in phrases like

'Look at that idiot, his tie's not straight.'

'That bloke next door really winds me up. Why can't he put his parting on the left side of his head like any other normal man?'

'Why do people insist on filling their car windows with stickers of all the places they've been to?'

The issues don't really matter. In fact, sometimes the more petty the issue is, the stronger they feel about it! If they do find something good to say, it usually has a hook.

'That was quite a nice meal darling, but couldn't you have made sure the cheesecake was totally defrosted before you served it?'

The fact that 'darling' may have slaved away in the kitchen for the last four hours bears no relevance!

The problem is that negative speech contaminates other people. In Hebrews 12:15 it says that when the root of bitterness springs up, it defiles many and causes trouble. One reason the children of Israel failed to enter the promised land was because of their grumbling and complaining. A friend of mine once said that The Church of Jesus Christ could make a major impact on the world if the individual members would stop grumbling and complaining like everyone else!

Gossip is easy to listen to unless you train yourself not to. It's so easy to take on board negative talk about others. It is sad but true that Christians are not immune to this sin.

'Yes you are right. The elders have done it again; made decisions and not asked us what we think.'

'Well the elders in the last church I was in were the same. In fact they used to ...'

'I don't suppose we'll find a church where the elders are any different.'

Birds of a feather flock together, so says the old proverb. Find one negative person and you are likely to find their friends are all negative too. They feed one another on their distorted perceptions and thinking.

2. What you do

Your behaviour and your lifestyle becomes negative. That is, it does not build up, but tears down. It becomes difficult to relate to people. People stay away **because** they don't want to get contaminated. Many aspects of life start to get affected.

Eating can be affected. 'Comfort eating' is an easy thing to slip into when there are still unresolved issues within. A dear lady I know used to eat a Mars Bar every night in bed. Then God dealt with her about some hurts from the past. She forgave and released a number of people who had hurt her. The Mars Bars stopped and she started to lose weight significantly.

I know a man who's ability to eat was a phenomenon! He was quite slim and certainly not overweight. He did not have hollow legs, so what happened to the vast amounts of food he could tuck away? Nervous energy burnt it up. The tumult within was so great, it sapped him of energy. It was as much as he could do to physically satisfy his hunger.

When energy is used up like that, creativity dwindles. The ability to think laterally gets submerged in the hurts that are mulled around on the inside. Much of this happens at a subconscious level.

Anorexia Nervosa, the eating disorder, in my view, comes from unresolved hurts deep within. Princess Diana made newspaper headlines with a speech to medical experts concerning her interest and insights into the causes of eating disorders, particularly among young people.

She said, 'Many would like to believe that eating disorders are merely an expression of female vanity – not being able to get into a size 10 dress.' She dismissed this idea and said, 'From early childhood many had felt they were expected to be perfect but didn't feel they had the right to express their true feelings to those around them – feelings of guilt, of self revulsion and low personal esteem, creating in them a compulsion to "dissolve like a Disprin" and disappear.'

Those who developed eating disorders found that by focusing their energies on controlling their bodies they had found a refuge from having to face more painful issues at the centre of their lives.

She said that everyone could have a part to play in preventing it happening. 'As parents, teachers, family and friends, we have an obligation to care for our children, to encourage and guide, to nourish and nurture and to listen with love to their needs in ways which clearly show our children that we value them. They, in their turn, will then learn how to value themselves.'

I remember being moved to tears while watching the film *The Karen Carpenter Story* a number of years ago. The power of the Carpenters' lyrics, music and harmonies delighted millions. But a comment by one music paper reporter who called her 'chubby', turned her against herself to the point that she determined to lose weight to become 'acceptable'. Her continual loss of weight damaged her heart and in 1983 she died of heart failure, aged 32. As a result the world was robbed of a great singer.

The sadness in my heart was not just that she abused herself in the way she did. At one point in the film, the Carpenter family were with a psychiatrist treating Karen. He said that a common element in all patients suffering from Anorexia Nervosa was a particular fear. That fear was this; that if they don't live up to family expectations, they are not going to be loved. 'Are you saying that we don't love Karen?' asked her mother. 'No,' came the reply, 'but have you told her that you love her?' The mother quickly replied, 'We don't do things that way, you show a person – you don't tell them all the time.' Sadly, that seemed to be the one thing Karen Carpenter needed.

Sleeping can be affected. When a person goes to bed they continually nurse and rehearse the hurt within. Sleep escapes them. They then become 'night owls', to ensure that when they go to bed, they actually are so tired, they have to sleep.

Emotional and physical 'burn out' comes from trying to keep all the plates spinning on the outside, and yet on the inside they are all crashing to the floor. As much as a person tries to rationalise the issues, they don't disappear. The results can be disastrous.

The physical effects can be numerous. The bitterness of the hurts within seep into a person's physical body. Ulcers, rheumatism, arthritis, gynaecological problems and cancer, can be caused by the root of bitterness.

I was out preaching in the street one day, saying that arthritis can be caused by bitterness, but Jesus can heal people. An elderly lady in the crowd came forward waving her walking stick at me and shouting aggressively, 'I'm not a bitter person! I just hope you get arthritis one day. You don't know anything!'

Everyone else in the crowd could see that this lady's problem was that she **was** deeply bitter. The physical effects in her life were obvious; gnarled hands, stooped body, and venom on her tongue. Yet her thinking had become distorted trying to cope with the pain within. The fruit of resentment was seen in her speech and her actions.

A friend of mine used to visit an 86 year-old lady who was crippled with arthritis and rheumatism. One day he asked her about her childhood. She could remember the time her mother had brought her sister a beautiful dress for her birthday. She could also remember, with feeling, that her mother had not done so for her. She told my friend, 'I've hated my mother and sister ever since.' She died a bitter, twisted old lady a few months later, having held on to unforgiveness for eighty years.

I was speaking at a young couples week-end a number of years ago and was asked to pray for a woman who had lost a baby over a year earlier. She had not been able to conceive since. She and her husband had been prayed for by the elders in their church, but nothing had changed. As we talked, it became apparent that she had become bitter towards God, and her husband.

We explained that there is **never** any reason to need to forgive and release God! He never does anything wrong. He never hurts people. He is intrinsically good. When we are hurt, both the hurts and the enemy twist our thinking to make us believe that God is not good.

We first asked her to forgive her husband there and then. She did so with tears. We then took her through a prayer of repentance for her bitterness towards God and her husband. We then prayed that God would again open her womb. A year later we heard that she was a mother again. Such is the power of forgiveness!

I am not saying all these physical problems are always caused by unforgiveness, but I am saying they can be. Bitterness seeks to affect every area of our life.

Whenever I am asked to pray for the healing of someone with a similar condition, I usually start by asking if they have any unforgiveness in their heart. If the condition is a recent development, are there any issues recently that have provoked unforgiveness? If the condition is longstanding or persistent, is there unforgiveness going back to when the condition first started?

A man was once asked by a friend if there was anything about him his wife did not like. After pausing for thought he said, 'Yes, there are just two things.' 'What are those?' his friend inquired. The man replied, 'Everything I say, and everything I do!' The fruit of resentment is like that. It affects everything we say and everything we do.

Chapter 9

The Torture Chamber

'In anger his master turned him over to the jailers to be tortured, until he should pay back all he owed. "This is how my heavenly Father will treat each of you unless you forgive your brother from your heart."'

(Matthew 18:34–35)

Jesus promised that if you do not forgive from the heart, the Father will hand you over to the torturers. That is New Covenant teaching as well as Old Covenant.

*'The L*ORD *will never be willing to forgive him; his wrath and zeal will burn against that man. All the curses written in this book will fall upon him, and the L*ORD *will blot out his name from under heaven. The L*ORD *will single him out from all the tribes of Israel for disaster, according to all the curses of the covenant written in this Book of the Law.'*

(Deuteronomy 29:20–21)

Which man is this referring to?

'Make sure there is no root among you that produces such bitter poison. When such a person hears the words of this oath, he invokes a blessing on himself and therefore thinks, "I will be safe, even though I walk in the

stubbornness of my heart." This will bring disaster on the watered land as well as the dry.'

(Deuteronomy 29:18–19)

What is the 'torture'?

These verses follow the curses that would come upon Israel if they chose not to obey the Lord. Is it not possible that the torture might be affliction, calamity, adversity and even sickness? I am not saying that God sends sickness. He does not. But as a method of getting us to repent of our unforgiveness, He is prepared to release us from His protection. As a result, we are open to demonic affliction and sickness.

Deuteronomy chapter 28 is amazing. Fourteen verses of the blessing of obeying the Lord are followed by fifty eight verses of the curses that would follow disobedience.

Galatians teaches us that,

> *'All who rely on observing the law are under a curse, for it is written: "Cursed is everyone who does not continue to do everything written in the Book of the Law."'*
>
> (Galatians 3:10)

but

> *'Christ redeemed us from the curse of the law by becoming a curse for us, for it is written: "Cursed is everyone who is hung on a tree."'* (Galatians 3:13)

It would be possible to argue, therefore, that if Christ bore all the curses of Deuteronomy 28, we do not have to bear them. But look at 1 John 1:9.

> *'If we confess our sins, he is faithful and just and will forgive us our sins and cleanse us from all unrighteousness.'* (1 John 1:9)

Cleansing from unrighteousness comes because of confession of sin. If we hold on to the sin of unforgiveness, neither confessing it nor repenting of it, then we will be unable to experience the healing and freedom Jesus won for us. Again let us remind ourselves of what Jesus taught:

> *'Forgive us our debts, as we also have forgiven our debtors. For if you forgive men when they sin against you, your heavenly Father will also forgive you. But if you do not forgive men their sins, your Father will not forgive your sins.'*   (Matthew 6:12, 14f)

If you do not repent and confess your unforgiveness, there is no righteousness and no cleansing for you in those areas of your life. You open yourself to the 'curses' of Deuteronomy 28; the 'torture' of Matthew 18.

Who are the 'torturers'?

We saw in an earlier chapter that the devil can gain a foothold (literally, a place) in our lives if we are angry and do not forgive those who caused our anger (Ephesians 4:26f). The use of the word devil here does not mean that Satan himself will personally gain a place in you. Devil here is a generic term for his evil minions, demons. We are used to hearing and using these kind of figures of speech.

Imagine a criminal saying to his accomplice, 'Look out! Here comes the law!' He is actually referring to a policeman, not to the whole judiciary.

'The Company has decided to give an extra days holiday to the workforce this year', means the directors of the company have made the decision.

The use of the word devil, therefore, must be determined by its context.

> *'Submit yourselves therefore to God. Resist the devil, and he will flee from you.'*   (James 4:7)

> *'Discipline yourselves, keep alert. Like a roaring lion your adversary the devil prowls around, looking for someone to devour.'*   (1 Peter 5:8)

The devil is not personally involved with every individual. Unlike God, who is omnipresent, the Devil is not. We do not expect Queen Elizabeth to stop her Royal car and give a motorist parked on a double yellow line a parking ticket. That work is delegated through an authority structure to traffic police. So it is with the devil.

Anger, therefore, which is not resolved through forgiveness, gives demonic powers, the 'torturers', access to our lives to afflict, attack and oppress us.

What kind of 'torture' can we be subject to?

The following is not a complete list, but Deuteronomy chapter 28 would suggest the following:
- Curses, confusion and rebuke in all you undertake
- Pestilence
- Consumption, fever, inflammation
- Blight, mildew
- Lack of rain, drought
- Boils, tumours, scabs and itch from which there is no healing
- Madness, blindness, bewilderment of heart
- Oppression, robbery with no-one to defend you
- Frustration
- Sores on the knees and legs
- You sow much but reap little
- The produce of the ground withers and dies
- Losing your children
- Aliens prosper while you suffer poverty
- You have to serve your enemies
- The 'up and in'ners become the 'down and out'ers
- Distress
- Severe and lasting plagues
- Miserable and chronic sicknesses
- Every kind of sickness and plague
- A trembling heart
- Failing eyes
- Despair of soul

– Your life shall hang in doubt before you
– You shall be in dread day and night

You could sum it by saying it's all **bad news**! Although people suffer these terrible tragedies, they never turn to God. They continue to do it 'My Way'. The curses mentioned above were to be released only upon those who rejected God's way and chose to go their way. Notice how many of the consequences of disobedience would affect their health.

Today, hospitals are filled with many people who are needlessly sick. It is estimated that 20% of all British hospital beds are taken by those with alcohol related problems. Why do people turn to alcohol? To numb the pain within. To help them cope with the disappointments and hurts that have come their way.

For others, the only answers for recurring sicknesses is treatment by drugs. The real cause is often undiscovered. Friends of mine who are doctors, tell me they see a continual stream of people whose health could change for the better if they were willing to forgive and release those who have hurt them.

A psychiatrist friend of mine often feels powerless with her patients. The reason is that the answer to many people's emotional and mental needs is not prescribed on the National Health Service.

Many people today are turning to alternative medicine. Mainstream medicine does not seem to come up with the goods for them. A major reason that practitioners of alternative remedies are getting more 'patients' is that they have 'time' for them. They will actually listen to them and try to understand the underlying issues.

Unfortunately, many people are still going to be sick even though they have had their feet rubbed, muscles tested, backs manipulated, bathwater smelling nice, legs crossed and mind emptied.

Why? Because they remain in the Torture Chamber of Unforgiveness.

Chapter 10

Open the Books

A Stubborn Heart

Some people make excuses for their lack of forgiveness.

'I could never forgive them for what they've done to me. It hurts too much.'

'I tried to once, but it didn't seem to make any difference.'

'Anyway, it's their fault ... They are the ones that have done wrong. They should be coming to me.'

These are all excuses of a stubborn heart. Remember what Deuteronomy 29 says about the bitter man? He walks in the stubbornness of his own heart. Saying 'I could never forgive' is being stubborn. It's opening the door to the torture chamber and closing the door on God to His forgiveness.

Do we sometimes wonder why we are constantly going into sin, constantly falling to temptation? Is it because there is no righteousness, there is no cleansing, there is no forgiveness because we have not forgiven others?

I have come across a number of Christians who deal with the hurts by saying,

'Well, I've tried to forgive six times already, but it keeps coming back. So I just keep on forgiving them, every time I think about it. Like Jesus said, seventy times seven.'

But this is **not** what the parable in Matthew 18 teaches. The parable teaches that you forgive the person and release them from the debt. When the account is settled, that is the end of the matter.

The King did not go out and have to forgive the servant again and again. Why? Because the account was settled once and for all. God does not have a 'record card' of all the wrong things we have done unless we are living with unforgiveness. We have a clean sheet. That is how He wants **us** to be. The point of the parable is that accounts were settled and closed.

God wants to set His people free. Most people, if not everybody, have been brokenhearted at some point in their life. That is why part of the commission of Jesus was to bind the broken hearts and set the captives free. Many people are captive to their emotions. They are frightened of letting them be exposed for fear of what might come out. But Jesus wants to set us free in every way.

'So if the Son sets you free, you will be free indeed.'
(John 8:36)

The Debtors

Here is list of the people who are the most likely to have hurt us and caused us to feel owed.

Father, Mother, brother, sister, child, auntie, uncle, grandfather, grandmother, friend, teacher, husband, wife, and if you are a Christian, church leaders.

In other words, all the people who tend to be close to us. The ones who should bring most security are often the ones who hurt us the most. Many of the hurts they have inflicted on us may have been unintentional, **yet they are real to us**. If they have not been dealt with, they can be as painful today as they were the day they happened.

The wife of a husband that has had an affair has been robbed. First, her husband has taken the love and affection that should have been given to his wife and given it to someone else. Secondly, the lover has robbed the wife of her husband. Both need forgiving and releasing.

The Debts

Although parables are not allegories in the strict sense, there is much that can be understood of forgiveness if we look closer at Matthew 18.

When the man who owed the king ten thousand talents came before him, the money the king was owed may have been made up of various items. 400 barrels of oil, 200 sacks of wheat, 20 donkeys etc. The king would have an account book showing entries or copies of the invoices, complete with dates and details of each transaction. Clearly the slave had not paid anything to the king at the time the king wished to settle accounts.

So it is within us. We keep records of the wrongs done against us, noting the who, when, where and how in our memory and emotions. As much as we try to bury the issues, rationalise them or just deny them, God has ways of calling us to account. My prayer is that the Holy Spirit will bring you illumination of any debts outstanding that have not been dealt with.

The Accuser

The brain has the capacity to not only recall memory but also to recall emotions that went with the memory. That is why nostalgia is big business. If we hear a song from the time we were pursuing a handsome young man or beautiful young lady, we don't just remember the words. We can remember the romantic feelings that we had at that time. We may well be able to feel our heart start to beat faster!

This is also true at a negative level. When the enemy comes to help us rehearse the hurts, he is never general. He doesn't say 'Well you just had a bad childhood.' The enemy of our souls can be as accurate as the laser-guided bombs we saw used in Iraq in the Gulf War. He will take the 'videotape' of our memory and spin it back to specific incidents. He will say:

'Do you remember the time when your mate broke your

bike. He didn't even offer to pay or mend it. He just laughed. So did Frank and John who were with him.'

The truth is this. Although we may be owed literally, inside we feel owed more because the laughter of those boys humiliated us. They robbed us of self-esteem. They made us feel powerless and pathetic. Inside that can still hurt. 'Do you remember when the headmaster told you that you would never pass any exams because "You're a waster."'

Those words can have seemed to be like a curse hanging over us for the rest of our educational life. When we failed our exams, we came to the conclusion that maybe the headmaster was right. We then started to believe him. 'I'm no good. I'm a failure. I'll never be good at anything.' The Accuser was always quick to agree.

Can you remember when your father or mother spoke out of frustration to you words that wounded you deep down on the inside. You can think about them right now and still feel how you felt then. You can feel the knot in your stomach, the tightness in your throat, the tear in your eye. At these times it is no good claiming 'It's all dealt with'. Your emotions know that these things are not resolved.

The Bully

At secondary school, a boy who was in my year had set about another boy with a belt and beaten him quite badly. The deputy head came to our Technical Drawing lesson to ask if anyone in the class knew who did it. The boy who had been attacked was too frightened to 'split'. I put my hand up amidst gasps from my form mates. They knew the consequences that I would face from the bully.

Several days later, on the school playing field, I was told, 'Eddy wants to see you.' I anxiously went across to see him. He put his face right up to my face.

'Wait till the end of term, Day. I'm going to get you!'

With that he head butted me, sending me reeling to the

floor. His mates jeered. My mates were surprised I got off so lightly. I lived in fear for the next four weeks unsure of what my fate would be at his hands.

I told nobody how scared I was. I bought a book on Judo and practised in my bedroom! I tried to convince myself I could beat him in a fair fight. The problem was, he didn't fight fair.

The last day of term came. I hadn't seen him all day, but knew he had been up to no good. I had done some serious praying that day even though I wasn't really walking with God at that time. I had my plan hatched. If he was there with his mates I would run. If he was there by himself I would fight. My heart was in my mouth as I walked to the school gates.

He never showed up at all. He was too busy letting down tyres in the school bike sheds.

I saw him again nearly ten years later, on a visit to my home town. He obviously didn't recognise me, but a chill went up my spine, and a knot came to my stomach when I saw him. Sometime later I heard that in a domestic dispute where he was drunk, he climbed over the balcony edge of his 5th floor flat, fell off and died.

When I heard that, I was glad. I remember saying to my brother, 'He finally got what he deserved.' I thought the issue was closed. Then God started to speak to me.

Mercy – the Key Factor

Grace, I was once told, is getting what we don't deserve, whereas mercy is not getting what we do deserve.

'Are you going to forgive him?' came the familiar voice into my spirit. 'But he's dead now, Lord.' 'You were robbed by him on that school field and you know it', came the reply.

I never had forgiven him. I thought it was just one of those experiences you went through. It toughens you up for the real world and helps to shape your character. I now thought back to those fourth form days. I not only felt angry at what he had done to me, but angry for the others he had hurt. I felt in my heart again the sense of injustice at how he had treated me and made me look weak and foolish. I also felt that he had robbed me of security. I had never known whether he would be waiting on the corner of my road when I got home from school.

Even though he was dead and buried, I knew I had unforgiveness in my heart towards him. That boy could never pay me back what he took from me. I forgave him specifically for the things he had done wrong to me. I also released him from what I felt he owed me in terms of self-esteem and security. I asked God for forgiveness for my unforgiveness and the bitterness in my heart.

Did he deserve it? No. I felt he deserved to have done to him what he had done to others. But neither did I deserve the forgiveness God gave me. God had mercy on me. He didn't give me what I really did deserve. It was because God had mercy on me, forgiving and releasing me, that I was able to do the same.

Releasing forgiveness to a dead man will not change him. But it changed me. I saw afresh the mercy of God.

It was Shylock in Shakespeare's *Merchant of Venice* that wanted his pound of flesh. We can be the same. We want what we are due. If we don't get it, we feel owed. We would like to get our own back on those who have taken from us and not returned. Choosing not to get our own back, but rather forgiving them, is having mercy.

The whole point of the parable is that the King had mercy. He did not give that slave what he should have had.

Who's to Blame?

There are some hurts that people take on board because of their own bad attitudes.

I remember hearing of a person who was praying through some issues of forgiveness, and saying, 'I want to forgive my sister for being better at school than me.' Fortunately, those who were praying with the person stopped them.

There was no need to forgive her sister. There was a need to repent of jealousy.

We are not just looking to put the blame for our bad attitudes on other people. We must take responsibility for our own sin and our own sinful attitudes. We must take responsibility for our own jealousy, our own selfishness, our own pride and repent and seek God's forgiveness. Neither should we excuse ourselves by blaming it on demons!

There are also times when we are genuinely hurt by people but they did not understand what they were doing. How many times when something has happened have we heard the words, 'Don't blame them, they didn't do it deliberately'. Yet inside we felt that they were responsible for what happened. It is quite possible for people to hurt us and sin against us unknowingly. When Jesus was on the cross, He said,

> *'Father, forgive them; for they do not know what they are doing.'*   (Luke 23:34)

If Jesus found it necessary to forgive those who did not understand what they were doing, how much more should we?

Chapter 11

Settling Accounts

How do you do it?

This is the part in the book where the 'we' becomes 'you'!

1. Prepare to do business with God

Ask the Holy Spirit to open up areas where your emotions have been damaged; where you feel **owed**; where you've been **hurt**. Maybe you can feel an ache in your heart right now. In your mind you could be saying, 'If only things could have been different; if only that didn't happen.' Hope deferred has made your heart sick.

You need to ask God to allow you to become 'connected' to the hurt and the pain in your heart. This is really important if you are to know God's healing on the inside. In fact, it is the only way you will actually be able to forgive **from the heart**.

If this becomes just an intellectual exercise, you may 'forgive' at a mental level, but leave your emotions unchanged. Your mind may have the satisfaction of knowing you have 'done the right thing', but the pain in your heart will remain and not get healed.

You may be the kind of person who 'rules' everything. When you pray, you will need to confess to the Lord any way you have 'excused' the injustices you have suffered. You will need to admit that you have suppressed or denied your feelings. This can be quite difficult. You will need someone else to pray with you to break down these defence mechanisms (strongholds). If you have been proud of your ability to handle situations in this way, you will need to repent of your pride too!

Why do some people find they are still hurting when they think about a person who they thought they had forgiven. There can be a number of reasons. Usually, it is because they mentally 'forgave' but it never touched their heart. Sometimes, there are still other issues with the person that need forgiving. Occasionally, the mind has chosen to 'block out' painful memories, and as a result forgiveness is not released into those areas. This is often true in cases of childhood trauma, e.g., sexual abuse.

The answer is to ask the Holy Spirit to reveal any unresolved issues. This is not 'navel' inspecting, it's account clearing!

2. *Make an invoice*

Get a piece of paper and write down a list of the people who have hurt you and what they did to hurt you. Don't rationalise ... 'It wasn't really my dad's fault' if inside you feel it was.

Be specific not general. e.g.,
Not:
>   Dad – for being a pain in the neck.

But:
>   Dad – for not encouraging me when I did well at school.
>   – constantly going on about my ears in front of others.
>   – never telling me he loved me.
>   – telling my friend I wet the bed
>   etc.

Making an invoice can be the first time we really come to terms with the hurt within and admit the fact that we are owed by others.

3. *Count the cost of releasing them*

Realise that they can never pay you back what you feel owed. The King knew that the servant was **unable** to pay, not just **unwilling**. In the same way, we could never 'pay back' what we owe to God. We could go to church every Sunday (and Wednesday). Have a quiet time every morning. Take communion every day. Give money to the poor. We could even go on the mission field, but we could never pay Him back.

It may be helpful at this point to think about how much God has forgiven you. When you became a Christian, you possibly said a 'prayer for salvation'. This probably included, what I call, 'blanket' words of repentance and forgiveness. In other words, we repent of everything generally and ask for forgiveness of everything generally. Although our heart may be genuine in this and we get born again, we miss the greatness of the grace of God. If we had a true understanding of what it cost God to forgive us each specific sin we had committed, the cost of forgiving others would seem insignificant by comparison.

Counting the cost also means no longer having an emotional weapon against the person who has hurt us. We once again become vulnerable to being hurt because our emotions are whole, not seared.

4. *Have mercy on them*

As you pray, acknowledge to God if you have felt that those who have hurt you deserve the same thing happening to them.

If they crashed your car, you may feel, or have felt that they deserve to have their car crashed. If they made fun of you and put you down in front of others, you may feel that is what should happen to them.

You may feel that they need to be made to feel how they made you feel. You may feel they actually deserve worse in return.

Determine that even if you had the person in front of you now, and had the power to do anything to them; you are going to show them mercy.

5. *Forgive and release them for each and every incident*

I have prayed through forgiveness with many people and heard them say, 'Lord I forgive my dad for not showing me love, for not encouraging me when I needed it.' They then go on to someone else, but I stop them.

I explain that it is good and right to forgive him, but there is a big hole in their heart, where they never had that love. When they never heard the words,

'Son I love you. Son I think you're tremendous. Son you really ride that bike well. Son I really appreciate you for just being you. There's nobody else like you in the whole world.'

There is a debt. There is a debt outstanding where those words which **should** have been spoken, never were. Why? Because fathers **should** say those things, even as the heavenly Father spoke to His Son. As a result, they need not only to **forgive** their father for the fact he did what he did, but they need to **release** him from the debt as well.

The King in Matthew 18 did not just forgive the man for not paying him the ten thousand talents he owed him. He actually released him from the debt as well.

For many people, praying through these kinds of issues can be quite traumatic and emotional. I personally feel it is better to have one or two Christian friends with you if you are going to be going through emotionally hurtful issues. They can encourage and help you to see things clearly.

They can also pray for you and help you to pray appropriately. They will also be witness to the fact that you have forgiven and released.

When you pray, speak out loud words like these:

'Father, in Jesus' name, I forgive (the person's name) for (the offence or list of offences) and the effect it has had on my life; and right now I release them from what they owe me.' Words have power. Proverbs 18:21 says:

> *'Death and life are in the power of the tongue ... '*

As you are praying out these things, you are speaking

powerful words that will break the power of the enemy's chains on your life. Cross out each item on your 'invoice' as you forgive and release the person.

Remember, if you pray 'Lord, this is the fifteenth time I've had to forgive them', then you did not forgive them the other fourteen times! Accounts are still open. If you keep score you have not forgiven.

Then ask God to forgive them and bless them. That kind of praying is powerful. It is also the test as to whether you have actually forgiven and released them.

> *'But I tell you who hear me: Love your enemies, do good to those who hate you, bless those who curse you, pray for those who mistreat you.'*   (Luke 6:27–28)

I have found tremendous personal release, having forgiven those who have mistreated me, by praying God's blessing on them. The enemy definitely does not like it!

6. *Ask God to forgive you for your unforgiveness*

While you had unforgiveness in your heart, there was no righteousness and no cleansing in that area. He can now forgive you on the basis of what Jesus said in Matthew 6:14:

> *'For if you forgive men when they sin against you, your heavenly Father will also forgive you.'*

7. *Get the person(s) with you to pray healing into your life*

> *'Therefore confess your sins to each other and pray for each other so that you may be healed. The prayer of a righteous man is powerful and effective.'* (James 5:16)

I cannot emphasise enough this scriptural injunction. Some people never get free from issues of unforgiveness because they have never confessed them to anyone else. They have kept it inside them. This is why it is good to have others with you to hear your confession.

Where you have been wounded emotionally, there will be need for healing. Just admitting you have been hurt does not bring healing. It just takes the sticking plaster off the wound. The person who is with you can lay hands on you and pray for you for this. It may be appropriate to pray for you after you have finished forgiving each person or each issue. As there may be a lot of emotion involved, this ministry should not be rushed.

Joel 2:25 says that God can restore (or make up) the years that the locusts have eaten. The locusts were a destructive army that the Lord was to release against His people because of their disobedience. The promise of God's Spirit being poured out on all flesh at the end of Joel 2, follows the call to repentance, and the promise of restoration.

God can restore the areas of your life where the enemy has eaten away at you emotionally and robbed you of righteousness and peace and joy. Those who are with you should pray this for you asking the Holy Spirit to come and refresh you and to fill you.

We have found that a person may need several hours to talk through the issues and pray. Sometimes, several sessions are needed. Those who are praying with and for another person need love, compassion and sensitivity. They must also be prepared to gently confront the person they are praying with if withholding of forgiveness or lack of repentance is evidenced. Healing is usually a process, but time is not the healer, God is. Jesus came to bind the broken hearts and to heal them.

8. *Tear up the invoice*

The account is now settled and closed. If the enemy ever comes back to you and says, 'Do you remember what that person did to you?' don't talk back to him. Turn your response into a prayer of thanksgiving. You can say;

'Yes, Lord. I remember the day when I wrote that down as a debt, and I forgave that person and I released them. They don't owe me a thing any more. Not only that, you have forgiven all my debts. You've had mercy on me. You've released me. Hallelujah!'

The Accuser will disappear quickly! Rejoice in God's goodness. Set your will to forgive and release any others that God shows you.

Chapter 12

Staying Free

All that we have looked at so far, I have called forgiving and releasing. But really, it is only **biblical** forgiveness. To forgive someone is to release them from the debt they owe. It is what the 'gospel' is all about. The Good News is that God has forgiven us because of Jesus. Our response is now to forgive those who have sinned against us. That is the practical implication.

It is tragic that many Christians believe that, but do not practice it. A person who says, 'Praise God I'm going to heaven now. I just hope that I don't have to spend eternity with **that** creep,' has not understood what Jesus had to say about forgiveness!

The whole concept of forgiveness in the Bible is to do with debts and debtors; having mercy on those that cannot pay back what they owe. Sadly, much Christian teaching on forgiveness has missed the vital aspect of **releasing** others as well as forgiving. That is one reason for writing this book. Another reason is so that new Christians can be given something to help them avoid the mistake of the unforgiving servant.

In our own church, as part of our 'new beginnings' course for new Christians, we devote a whole session to forgiving and releasing. At an early stage, these new believers get to clear out years of garbage the enemy has dumped on them. We have found that it sets a foundation of forgiveness in their spiritual life, which enables them to make good strides forward in their walk with God. Of course, this does not make them perfect overnight!

We train our people how to minister this to others. They are all keen. They know what a dynamic effect it has had on their own lives. (The final chapter of this book includes some of their testimonies.)

Sometimes, in ministering to people, the strongholds of unforgiveness seem to find physical expression under the power of the Holy Spirit's presence. This may include: pains in the stomach; the sense of being strangled (particularly when it actually comes to speaking the words of forgiveness); burping and belching; yawning; shaking; falling over; crawling around the floor; as well as weeping and loud cries of anguish. These strongholds can be broken through prayer.

In this 'clean up' process, we frequently come across demons. Some manifestations mentioned above may indicate demonic activity, but discernment and sensitivity to the Holy Spirit is needed. Sometimes the demons reveal their work as anger, hatred, rejection, jealousy, pride, and similar negative characteristics. They are confronted and cast out. It is beyond the scope of this book to deal with the casting out of demons.

People who have been 'chronic seekers' of the baptism of the Holy Spirit have often found it was unforgiveness that was the blockage. Those who have sought the Lord for healing and found none sometimes find that there is unresolved unforgiveness in their past that they were not consciously aware of. Their releasing forgiveness to others and receiving forgiveness themselves has been the key to their healing.

How to stay free

1. You must set your will to forgive and release anyone who has hurt or offended you, whether past or present

Not only that, you must make a quality decision of the will

to forgive anyone that hurts or offends you in the future, however great or small the offence.

At one time, major changes were about to take place in my life. I knew that I was going to face a time of conflict and confrontation with people I both loved and respected. Whilst praying one day, I felt the Lord say to me, 'Even if they drive a ten ton truck over you, you must let them. You must not fight them; they are your brothers. You must only pray for them and bless them. I will use the circumstances to shape your character, and develop greater faith in me.' The following 12 months were the most difficult of my whole life.

I had to encounter accusation both openly and behind my back. I had to face criticism, some of which was justified, and some of which was unjustified. Many things that were said wounded me deeply. I was not alone in this. My wife, too, had her fair share of 'going through the mill'. But in it all, we were determined to do what God had said, forgive, release and bless those who hurt us.

At one particular confrontation, I was told all the things I had not done and all the things I never would do. This left me feeling that the ten ton truck had been driven over my emotions, stopped, reversed back over me, put into forward gear and driven over me again! I remember sliding under the door that I had walked through thirty minutes earlier!

I had an underlying belief that these people were actually for me. It just did not feel like it at the time! I also had a few friends who really knew what I was going through. They helped me to sort out the wheat from the chaff and encouraged me to continue to forgive and to bless. They were also able to pray for me and minister healing to me as I have described previously.

God really did use the whole episode to strengthen my faith and my emotions. It again confirmed to me personally, the real power of forgiveness.

Determine right now, before the Lord, that you too, are going to set your will to forgive and release others.

2. *Get to work on the soil of insecurity in your heart*

A gardener will rake over his soil to remove any lumps of stone or debris that would stop his plants from having a firm foundation for their roots. He will also dig in manure to enrich it. Find the areas in your life where you are insecure. Most of us are a mixture of security and insecurity in differing degrees. We may feel secure in one setting but not in another. If you are not sure where you are insecure, ask your best friend!

All soil is susceptible to weeds. There is a story of a young minister who went to visit an old man. As he walked up the path to the cottage door, he admired the superb garden. It was beautifully laid out and well stocked with flowers. His opening gambit was to say, 'I see that the Lord has given you a beautiful garden.' 'Yes,' came the quick reply, 'but you should have seen it when it was left to him!'

If we do not attend to the garden of our heart, it is easy for the weeds to grow. They will choke the good seed that God wants to put in. We must diligently nurture the soil so that the good seed can produce a bumper crop of righteousness.

3. *Root out unbelief from your heart*

This must start by laying the axe to the root of any thinking pattern you have adopted that is contrary to the word of God. 2 Corinthians 10:4f talks about fortresses or strongholds of the mind. These lofty things are raised up against the knowledge of God. They can be destroyed by the weapons of our warfare, prayer and the word of God.

Romans 10:17 says that faith comes by hearing. Although the context here is to do with faith for salvation, the principle holds true in other areas. The verb 'hearing' is in the present continuous tense. This would allow us to interpret the text by saying, faith comes by hearing and hearing and hearing (i.e., continually hearing).

If you have been constantly told that you are useless, you can end up believing it is true, putting your faith in the fact of it being true, and finally living like it is true. But that thinking and that believing is directly contrary to the word of God! We must 'feed' the soil of our heart with the word of God. It is true that God has chosen the foolish, weak, base and despised things of the world (1 Corinthians 1:27f), but what does verse 30 say?

> '*It is because of him that you are in Christ Jesus, who has become for us wisdom from God – that is, our righteousness, holiness and redemption. Therefore, as it is written: "Let him who boasts boast in the Lord."*'
>
> (1 Corinthians 1:30–31)

4. Develop your personal relationship with the 'Gardener'

Many books have been written on this subject. The key is understanding the difference between knowing about God and knowing God. Some people could tell you so many details about the British Royal family that you would think that they knew the Queen personally. In reality they may have never met or spoken to any of them. Many Christians know lots of details about God, but don't really know Him personally.

Worship, Bible reading, prayer and fellowship with other believers are all important and necessary to our Christian growth. But don't be deceived into thinking those activities **are** our relationship with God. Sometimes they can be a substitute for the real thing. Knowing God is not to do with technique, it has to do with time. The way you really get to know Him is by spending time with Him. That time may not necessarily mean doing any of the above activities.

Communicate with the Lord constantly, whether you are walking down the street, driving the car, hanging out the washing or taking a bath. You can be conscious of His felt presence with you on a daily and hourly basis. If you have a daily 'devotional' time, it should be the cream on the cake of your relationship with the Lord, not the cake itself. The best times of intimacy in a marriage come as a result of good communication throughout the hours and days preceding.

5. *Sow the good seed of the word of God into your prepared soil*

We are now 'in Christ'. Find the book of Ephesians and highlight or underline all the verses that tell us who or what we are 'in Christ' or 'in Him'. Find the verses that tell you what He is in us. Turn these scriptures over in your mind again and again and again. It will be like turning over 'spiritual fertiliser' into the soil of your heart.

If you have been fed worry, anxiety and fear all your life, take time to read Matthew 6:25–34. Three times Jesus tells us 'Do not be anxious.' There are wonderful promises here that Jesus made to all those who are prepared to put His kingdom first their lives.

Matthew 5:23–26 gives Jesus' way of reconciling two Christians. If you realise there is an issue between you, go and get it sorted straight away. But there are ways of handling conflict that can cause hurt. I remember someone coming up to me at the end of a meeting where I had just preached.

'Joff, I just want you to know that I have really forgiven you for what you did to me.' I couldn't even think of having spoken to the man for several weeks. 'Oh, what was that?' I replied. 'You didn't smile back at me when I smiled at you last Sunday. I felt really hurt, but I forgave you this morning,' came the response.

I replied as best I could, 'Well, I think you could have got that sorted out between you and the Lord.' I didn't have time to talk to him about his insecurity, bad attitudes and other hangups. He went off feeling fine. I went off feeling that I needed to forgive him for being so stupid!

It is not always necessary to actually confront the person who has hurt you. This is especially true if they **do not know** they have hurt you. In fact confronting them may cause more hurt and bad feeling. But there are times where we must leave our 'offering' and go to see the person with whom we have an issue.

This kind of forgiving lifestyle is the essence of authentic Christianity.

Chapter 13

Forgiveness Brings Healing

1. Healing for the individual

This healing starts with the restoration of our broken relationship with God through repentance and faith. (See Appendix A.) We have also seen that having been forgiven by God, we must then forgive and release others. As we do this we are released from the 'torturers' who may have brought assorted problems into our lives. Healing, whether emotional or physical, can then be effected in our lives by the power of the Holy Spirit.

2. Healing for the family

Most family rifts continue because the members are unwilling to forgive and release those who have hurt them. The resulting 'feuds' can continue for generations. Each succeeding generation is fed with anger towards and hatred for the other side. This need not continue this way, or even start.

Parents must teach their children the principles of forgiveness from an early age. We have sought to help our children do this in two ways. First, if Elaine and I cause hurt to each other when the kids are around, we don't just 'make up' at bedtime. The kids get to hear us ask for and receive forgiveness from one another. This can be very humbling! Secondly, as a result of seeing daddy eating humble pie and apologising, they can be taught **why** he did.

As a result, they are learning how to release forgiveness to each other when they are wronged. They have also learned how to say sorry and ask for forgiveness when they have wronged someone else. This has helped to create an environment in our home where there are no 'undercurrents' of bitterness.

At school too, they are able to put into practice what they have learned at home. With the inevitable hassle of relating to peers, there is plenty of opportunity for forgiving and releasing! This has not made them weak or soft, though. Their ability to handle conflicts while they are young is building solid character into their lives.

As parents, therefore, we must not only teach, but model forgiveness for our children.

3. Healing for the local church

There is not one local church that does not at some time have hassle between its members. This is because the local church is made up of people! In some churches, unresolved issues have caused division and led to the church splitting. There is often much heartache and bitterness as a result. The resulting church factions may fail to grow significantly because of their unforgiveness of each other.

Many such conflicts could be resolved if churches and individual Christians would obey the Bible. Jesus gave some clear instructions about handling such conflict.

> *'You have heard that the ancients were told, "You shall not commit murder" and "Whoever commits murder shall be liable to the court." But I say to you that everyone who is angry with his brother shall be guilty before the court; and whoever shall say to his brother, "Raca," shall be guilty before the supreme court; and whoever shall say, "You fool," shall be guilty enough to go into the fiery hell.*

If therefore you are presenting your offering at the altar, and there remember that your brother has something against you, leave your offering there before the altar, and go your way; first be reconciled to your brother, and then come and present your offering.

Make friends quickly with your opponent at law while you are with him on the way, in order that your opponent may not deliver you to the judge, and the judge to the officer, and you be thrown into prison. Truly I say to you, you shall not come out of there, until you have paid up the last cent.'   (Matthew 5:21–26)

The implication in these verses is that a brother has something against you, because of something you have said or done. As you are doing some 'spiritual' activity, you are reminded of the fact. Jesus said that it is then your responsibility to go and get things put right ... even if it means missing the start of the Sunday meeting or Wednesday evening Bible study.

Once more we see Him referring to the **prison** and by implication the **prison officer** (jailer of Matthew 18), as well as the fact that you have not **paid up**. These are all phrases we are familiar with.

It seems here, that if you know someone has unforgiveness towards you, and you are not prepared to get it sorted, God will deal with you as well as them. They may have been delivered over to the jailers because of their unforgiveness towards you. If you do not get the situation resolved though, you could be heading for the jail as well!

Sometimes relationships get broken because of:
– a careless attitude
– misunderstanding
– non-communication
– sin

but, it is your responsibility to get it resolved.

Before the parable of the unforgiving servant in Matthew 18, Jesus gives similar instructions to the ones above.

> *'And if your brother sins, go and reprove him in private; if he listens to you, you have won your brother. But if he does not listen to you, take one or two more with you, so that by the mouth of two or three witnesses every fact may be confirmed. And if he refuses to listen to them, tell it to the church; and if he refuses to listen even to the church, let him be to you as a Gentile and a tax-gatherer. Truly I say to you, whatever you shall bind on earth shall be bound in heaven; and whatever you loose on earth shall be loosed in heaven.'*
>
> (Matthew 18:15–18)

If you become aware that your brother has sinned, what is your responsibility? It is not to go the church leaders and tell them; not at this stage anyway. Go to the person in private. Often our own hangups and fear of rejection will try to prevent us doing this, but do it we must.

Jesus then says what to do if you are not received by the person. Only after that step does the issue become one for the church leadership. Notice too, that what Jesus said regarding binding and loosing was to do with forgiveness. Although it may also refer to church discipline, He was saying that if you refuse to release forgiveness here, it will not be released in heaven. But if you forgive and release here on earth, it will be forgiven and released in heaven. This is how we can understand what Jesus said in Matthew 6:14f.

> *'For if you forgive men for their transgressions, your heavenly Father will also forgive you. But if you do not forgive men, then your Father will not forgive your transgressions.'*

4. Healing for the Body of Christ

It is estimated that there are some 22,000 denominations across the world, and the number is growing. This does rather seem to contradict the prayer of Jesus in John 17.

*'I do not ask in behalf of these alone, but for those also who believe in Me through their word; **that they may all be one**; even as Thou, Father, art in Me, and I in Thee, that they also may be in Us; that the world may believe that Thou didst send Me.'* (John 17:21f)

22,000 does not equal one! However there can be diversity as well as unity. Sadly, many Christians in one stream or denomination look at those in another with fear and suspicion. For some the fear is real because they have been hurt by some of those others.

Again, the answer is the same. Those that have caused hurt must be forgiven and released. This must take place first with church leaders. They themselves must forgive and release those who have hurt and wounded them, if they are to bring their churches into freedom. This will not resolve the many theological and doctrinal differences that separate groups. However, it will pave the way for relational reconciliation. Forgiveness is the very heart of Christianity.

5. Healing for the world

The 'United' Nations are constantly looking for ways to bring resolution to troubled areas of the globe. The peace negotiators struggle to reconcile opposing factions. Their task grows tougher each day. Constantly they are seeking answers. Are there any?

In April 1992, 600 people went on a prayer walk of reconciliation from St Paul's Cathedral, London to the Brandenburg Gate in Berlin. When two men, N.J. 'Mac' McCarthy and Charles Simpson heard about it quite separately, they decided to go too.

Mac MacCarthy flew over 30 missions to Germany and the occupied countries of Europe during the Second World War. As well as military targets, the brief was to carpet bomb civilian cities. Four of the raids were on Berlin. At the time, he rationalised his actions. His own parents had been bombed out, and it seemed necessary to win the war.

After the war, he met a German prisoner in a village shop. Mac was still in uniform and the prisoner asked him in a broken English accent, 'You bomber?' 'Yes,' Mac replied. 'You bomb Essen?' 'Yes, three times,' Mac replied. Tears came to the man's eyes. 'I live in Essen,' he said. Mac was touched very deeply, and that meeting started him on a path to seek reconciliation with those he had once bombed.

In 1971, Mac became a Christian following a heart attack and subsequent divine healing. In the autumn of 1991 he felt God say two things to him. Seek reconciliation and go to Berlin. He did not know how he was to do these two things until he heard about the Prayer Walk of Reconciliation to be held in the April of the next year.

Charles Simpson's story was quite different. His ship was blown up by the Germans during the war and he lost many friends and colleagues. He was one of the survivors.

Many years later, he realised that as a Christian, he could no longer hold on to any grievance or prejudice. He realised that because of what Jesus did at the Cross, unforgiveness was the biggest sin to hang on to. On his 78th birthday, he started the 820 mile walk to Berlin with Mac and 600 others.

Along the way, the organisers held 'prayer concerts' at various towns and in the different countries. At each concert the purpose of the walk was spelled out. On many occasions, Mac and Charles shared the reasons that they were there. Mac was seeking forgiveness. Charles had come to forgive.

At the end of each evening the audience were invited to respond. At one particular church in Germany, several hundred people attended. As people were invited to respond, they thought that only a few of the older people might come up. In fact the whole church got up and came forward! Many were saying how relieved they were that forgiveness was possible after all the time that had elapsed.

The final rally at the Brandenberg Gate, to quote Mac was, 'Totally crazy. I don't know how many Germans I hugged and kissed that day. It was wonderful.'

If both of these stories could be repeated all over the world, then reconciliation would surely come. Maybe revival would follow. Many people still hold on to bitterness and unforgiveness towards old enemies. This is particularly true of the victims of the two world wars. Some who were never born then, have taken on board the hatred from their forebears. The rise of neo-Naziism is only one example.

A new generation is arising, however, who are not prepared to just 'paper over the cracks' and 'let bygones be bygones'. This is a generation of people who have met One who has had mercy on them when they did not deserve it. He forgave them and released them from every debt of the past. They are now setting their hearts to do to others what has been done to them.

Will you join them?

Chapter 14

It Really Works!

Forgiving and releasing is not 'the latest thing'. Neither is it a formula or technique. It is doing what Jesus told us to do. Having been forgiven and released by God ourselves, we forgive and release others.

It is **settling accounts**. Some of those accounts may go back a long time. For some, therefore, this may be a long process. For others not so long. Often it is like peeling off layers of an onion. You finish one layer, and another begins! Having started the process though, it is worth pressing through to the end. Don't give up. Don't feel this will never end. God will give you grace.

It is not just those who have had an unhappy or unstable family background that need to forgive. We have all sinned and have all been sinned against. That is why Jesus came into the world. If we all **need** forgiveness, then we all **need** to forgive.

If the thought of forgiving those who owe you seems daunting, take courage from the following stories. None of them are 'super-testimonies'. That's the reason they are included. We can so easily feel that we need to be a super-sinner rather than just an ordinary Christian to need to experience any kind of 'inner' healing. This just isn't the case. They are ordinary people sharing how forgiveness has changed their lives. If being forgiven by God changed you, so will forgiving others. It really works!

Robbed of self-confidence

One evening God reminded me of an incident that happened when I was fifteen years old. Four other girls and I used to do everything together. Then Paula, the 'leader of the pack', began to date Kevin. I told her that he was no good for 'us', as he was into drugs, sex etc.

The next day I received a letter from the others informing me of **all** my faults. These ranged from having bad breath to my bras were too big; from Brad never did kiss me (he wouldn't go near me with a barge-pole), to I needed to see a psychologist.

I took the letter home and showed it to my mother. Her response was, 'Your sister and I were talking the other day and **we** think you need a psychologist too!' My dad's response was, 'I told you Paula is a two-faced bitch.' All I wanted was some encouragement, but I didn't get any.

That evening I remonstrated to God, 'But I have forgiven them.' He replied, 'Yes but you haven't released them.' I thought for a moment and asked, 'What do they owe me?' 'They owe you twenty years of self-confidence and self-esteem', He replied.

I welled up with the deepest sense of being owed. It was incredible. Then I was flooded with emotion and an awareness of injustice and unrighteousness. I also knew that what they had taken from me they could never pay back or restore. I knew I felt owed. I prayed and released them and was then overwhelmed with a personal sense of release. It was wonderful! Now I know that I am released from the effect of having no self-confidence and no self-esteem. Glory to God!

Robbed of a husband

Five weeks after my wedding day I discovered that my husband was having an affair. I was devastated and in the days that followed, my feelings towards the girl became increasingly violent. I was full of anger and hate towards her. During the next fortnight my husband decided to make an effort to mend our marriage. He returned home, but the damage had been done. I never trusted him again, and this incident along with others finally resulted in our divorce.

My feelings of hate towards my husband's girlfriend continued to smoulder and eat away at my heart. Each time I passed her house I radiated hostility toward it! Each time I saw her in town, my hatred would boil up on the inside and I would find swear words directed at her involuntarily coming to my lips. I would have to cross the road to avoid looking at her. I felt that I could have so easily hit her.

This situation continued for some years. During this time, I felt like I had been turned over to the jailers to be tortured as a result of my unforgiveness. I knew that Jesus' command was to forgive others. But it was not until the poison inside me reached an unbearable intensity one day that I realised that forgiving this girl (impossible though it seemed) was my only option. It had to be done and needed determination and self-discipline on my part.

I first prayed for God's help, then forgave the girl and released her from robbing me of my husband. Within minutes of praying and forgiving, I felt a great peace flooding into me and replacing the turmoil. I could hardly believe that this inner change was so real. I could hardly wait to bump into this girl in town to see how I would react towards her. I knew that it would be then whether my heart had really changed.

In fact I did not see her for 2–3 months, but the peace remained and I was able to drive past her house quite comfortably. Then I met her in the supermarket!

There we were, advancing inescapably towards each other up the aisle, trolleys laden with no way out. To my amazement and with no forethought and no effort on my part, I found myself walking up to her with a smile on my face! I greeted her warmly and inside I felt like I was giving her a hug. God's love inside me just overflowed outwards towards her. I am not sure which one of us was most surprised.

A while later, we met again in similar circumstances and again I found myself greeting her warmly. This time, however, I asked her forgiveness for all the hurtful things I had said to her at the time of the affair. This just seemed to complete the healing that God was doing within me.

God really honoured my decision to obey His word. The part I played in forgiving and releasing was so small compared with what He did. In taking away all my hatred and replacing it with His love and warmth, I became a different person.

Robbed of a father's approval

The love from my parents was always implied but rarely physical in terms of hugs and kisses. This coupled with sentiments of 'big boys don't cry' and 'be a man' had a detrimental effect on my emotional development. What was really being said was 'don't show them at any cost'.

My father frequently put his work before my achievements. Having spent sixteen weeks going through the Metropolitan Police Training school, I passed all my exams and became a Police Constable. He didn't even turn up for my passing out parade. The event became a non-event to me.

Something that helped me understand how I got hurt and the process of forgiving and releasing is that of an elastic band held at both ends and twisted until knots have appeared. The twisting represents the hurts, let downs and building up of inner tension over the years. It follows that a reverse process has to take place in order to get back to normality both emotionally and spiritually. Speaking out, 'I forgive you' sometimes isn't enough. We can all make mental decisions to say things, that can be quite independent of how the heart feels. But when the heart is involved, there is a difference.

The next stage is the release part. For me I hugged my parents for the first time. I knew when I had done this that the release had come. The look on their faces was wonderful!

I am now really aware that whenever my elastic band starts to get wound up, I can forgive and release and be free.

Robbed of adulthood

Talking with a friend one day, I realised that I had grown up physically, but not emotionally and mentally. I spent the whole of my adolescence believing I was evil and that nobody, not even God, loved me. Also that I had to look after myself because nobody else would. That I could only trust myself and nobody else. That at no cost could I let go of the hurt emotions inside of me. I could not accept the womanhood that God gave me, because I couldn't let go of the childhood I'd never had.

As I started to pray, I found I couldn't. Then the emotion started to pour out. All the pain, all the hurt, all the injustice. I didn't want to forgive, I didn't want to let go, I didn't want to cancel the debt. I wanted back what I was owed.

I felt wrecked. I knew that all the tears and cries were the cries of the hurt child still within me. Gradually the crying subsided. As I prayed, I forgave and cancelled the debt I felt each person owed me. I accepted the fact that I couldn't go back to my childhood again, and gave it to God. In a 'picture', I saw the struggle, the pain and the crying child recede away from me. I knew that my childhood had finally been laid to rest.

I was so exhausted after this experience that I went home and fell asleep. When I awoke I was overcome by joy at the fact that God had totally changed my life! I was not the person I had been in the morning. I felt a completely different person. No longer a child, but a woman ... the woman God wanted me to be.

Forgiving yourself

When I was in my early twenties, I had an abortion. The trauma was so great that I took an overdose of tablets and was admitted to hospital. Over the following years, although I knew I had done something terribly wrong, I didn't let my conscience get the better of me. I squashed down inside me the pain and guilt I felt. I also got married, had a child and got divorced.

What I hadn't bargained for was that my guilt and the inability to forgive myself started showing in other ways. For no apparent reason, I developed a number of chronic ailments. I started eating compulsively when I wasn't hungry. I developed an overwhelming fear of getting cancer and dying, and losing my children in the same way. I felt condemned, and different to everyone else. I started to see myself as a totally worthless person. More worrying to me than that was that I felt as if something inside me was dead. It felt like a sort of blank space where something important ought to be.

I carried these things with me for a long time. When I became a Christian, friends started to pray with me and showed me how to forgive and release all the people in my life who had hurt me. Although this had a good effect on me, I still wasn't free from the negative feelings and felt separated from God.

One day a friend of mine said that she sensed that I felt a very great need to be punished for something I had done. Her words shook me to the core and I immediately burst into tears – most unusual for me! I knew instantly what the issue was, and all the pain and guilt came to the surface. I had never forgiven myself. I knew I ought to, but felt that what I had done was so terrible that I could not let Jesus bear it for me, I deserved the punishment myself. For two weeks I cried – gut wrenching sobs as I repented and faced up to what I had done and how I had grieved God.

As I prayed again with friends, someone showed me that although God had forgiven me, I had never received His forgiveness for this issue. Then I found the key that unlocked the door for me. I didn't have to ask Jesus to take my punishment, He had already taken it, 2000 years ago. He carried my sorrows and my pains so that I don't have to. With relief I was able to say the words I needed to say – that I forgave and released myself.

I was unprepared for what happened next. I had a clear picture of a mocking, demonic figure standing between me and God. It was a spirit of death that had had me in its grip for years. No wonder I felt dead inside. It was reluctant to leave, but was banished after a struggle. I then felt a great tingling in my arms and hands, and found myself kneeling down, head on the floor with my hands outstretched. I then received what felt like a torrent of gold dust being poured into my hands. It was a cleansing and refining process, a precious outpouring of God's forgiveness that I was now able to receive. I was reminded of the words of Psalm 24 that I could now *'ascend the hill of the Lord'* with *'clean hands and a pure heart'*.

The next week of my life was incredible. The fear of death relating to me and my family had gone. The feelings of unworthiness were replaced by a sense of being arrayed in shining gold. The pain that had been within had just melted away. The sense of condemnation left me as did the deadness inside. I felt as if I had woken up after a long sleep! I also found that I could easily forgive others as I had received God's forgiveness for myself.

A problem with men

My dad had a drink problem when I was a child. This meant my early days were full of promises made when sober, but broken when he was drunk. I grew up learning to distrust him. Both my parents told me big girls don't cry, and as I was the eldest I should set an example. I can remember running to my bedroom and forcing myself not to cry when I was hurt. I even spoke to myself in the mirror saying I hated myself for crying.

Another occasion when I used to tell myself I hated me was after my dad would smack me for doing wrong. He would go on about it for weeks. Nothing I could say or do would help. It was then I thought that I must be horrible and unlovable as he was always right. Things got so bad that after one incident where he told someone else in the family about something I had done, I carved, 'I hate my dad' in the stairs. I didn't care if he found it because he could then smack me again and I felt I deserved it as I was so horrible. I would always struggle and strive to please people and earn their acceptance.

When I was fourteen a man tried to rape me. This reinforced my negative view of men. I later married a man who turned out to be so much like my dad that I panicked and fought him. This finally ended our often, very violent marriage. My whole experience of men had been that of violence, frustration and fear. I would almost do anything to keep the peace and ended up a 'doormat' as a result. I would even get panic attacks and leave trolleys full of shopping in the supermarket.

The only time I received attention when I was young, was when I was ill. So I made myself sick and ill to get attention. When my marriage broke up, I felt so guilty and a failure that I became ill and needed major surgery. My life was a mess!

When I became a Christian, my life changed, but everything did not get sorted out. I understood about forgiving, but did not understand about releasing. I 'forgave' all the people I could think of because I knew it was what God wanted. It was sometime later, though, that I understood the wonderful truth of forgive and release.

It has taken me months to work through the issues of forgiveness in my past, but God has done many wonderful things in my life over those months. I have been healed from a cyst in the womb as well as heartburn and indigestion which I had for years. My relationship with my new husband has grown into something I could never have imagined. We are so much closer. I can trust him now, not because he's different, but because God has changed me. I really feel I can be me now ... it really doesn't matter if I get things wrong. I have seen God's love in a new way.

Sucker for a lost cause

After being a Christian for more than two years, I found myself in quite a 'dry' period. The Lord was still working in many areas of my life, but emotionally I was in turmoil. Someone suggested that I was spending too much time with men, having them round the house all the time. I was quite offended but prayed and asked the Lord to show me if it was right. I was starting to feel very touchy and was near to tears quite a lot for no particular reason. I asked some Christian friends to pray with me. I assumed that it was tied up with my two failed marriages, but it wasn't. It was much earlier than that.

When we started praying, the Lord took me back to times in my childhood where I had to tell 'white' lies. This was because my father wanted me to cover up some problem at home that 'no-one need know about'. Also at other times I was given the responsibility of looking after my sisters, running the home etc.. My father would command that things were to be done in a certain way. I felt that anything I did was never good enough as he constantly criticised me and what I did. I forgave and released my dad for all the times he had done this and for the debt I felt owed for failing to say the words 'I love you'.

I also forgave my brother. I realised that he had hurt me as well. He was always making horrible comments about me when I was younger. I was called 'fatty', 'tubs' or 'blubber'. It may have seemed like Northern humour at the time, but it hurt me deeply.

I also always felt guilty. Silly though it may sound, I would confess to things that I hadn't done. This went back to my childhood and early teens. My brother would never admit to breaking things. My parents would make us stand and constantly question and shout until one of us admitted to the 'crime'. Because I couldn't stand the bad feelings that went with this, I would 'own up' just to keep the peace. I prayed and forgave my parents and my brother. The release from my guilty emotions was amazing. The hardest one of all, however, was yet to come.

I had always idolised my mother for being the 'rock' in our family. Whenever everything seemed to fall apart, mum was there, always available. My parent's marriage was awful for years and years, but my mum kept on a brave face. Although my father was not physically violent, he was harsh and cruel with his words. He would come and go as he pleased with no respect for my mum. Even after he left

111

her for the fifth time, she still had him back. Then in my early teens 'he' decided to move from one end of the country to the other, taking the family with him and leaving me. I wasn't consulted at all. As a result I felt that I had lost my mum and my two little sisters who I'd spent years looking after. My mum just let it happen.

As my friends were praying with me, I realised that my mum wasn't so perfect after all. I forgave her and let the Lord come and heal those areas. I now realise that this had affected the whole of my adult life. I had picked totally unsuitable partners and had surrounded myself with male friends because I was trying to earn some sort of standing with them. I had always been a 'sucker for a lost cause'. As the Lord brought healing into my heart I felt quite different.

I still want to help 'lost causes' now, but for God – not so that I feel useful. I know that I'm no longer a 'soft option' for others to lean on. Over the last six months, the Lord has helped me build some really good friendships with other women in the church. I also realise that the change has to be active on my part – not passive. I have managed to break with people I knew were using me.

I'm happy now to take time with the Lord – I was a Martha not a Mary. I know there are still things God wants to change, but now feel I'm well on the way. After years of feeling bad about myself and wanting to look like or be like others, I actually like being me. It's amazing!

A heart transplant

It was March 1990. I was exhausted. Physically I had a chest infection; emotionally I had put the lid on hurts from my past and spiritually our church had just gone through a very acrimonious split.

We were at the Laying On Of Hands 'Foundation Class' in the church and I finally gave up striving and admitted to God I couldn't make it on my own any more. Someone brought a prophetic word that God wanted me to be like Mary and not like Martha. That really hit the nail on the head! I had been struggling on, wanting to serve others, and kidding myself I was alright. All I really wanted to do was cry.

God was very gracious to me over the next few months and prepared me for what was to be a major operation. My 'anaesthetic' was to be 'slain in the Spirit' each Sunday meeting for most of the worship time – usually with no one laying hands on me! Whilst on the floor I kept experiencing God's unconditional love and surrendered myself to Him to change me.

At a conference I attended later that year, God gave me a picture of me undergoing an operation – it was a heart transplant. I was in theatre and could see the surgeon's eyes. They were full of compassion. I knew that it was Jesus. During the week, I had an excruciating pain in my left shoulder. After some prayer, I fixed up to see one of the church leaders and his wife. They asked me to make a list of those I felt owed me.

After the conference, I made the list, which was not very long, but covered some major issues. My parent's marriage broke up at the time I was 19 and left home for university. Sadly, communication had broken down long since. They had shown me a pretence of marriage but with no open display of affection to me or each other.

This came in to sharp relief one day. We phoned some friends to say that we were going to be in the area and pop in for a cup of tea. She said that her and her husband had separated. I was completely stunned as everything had seemed OK with them. She told me that it was 'one of those things' and that there was no-one else involved. They had felt it better to separate while they were still 'friends'. I was devastated and couldn't sleep for the next two nights. My husband and I realised that my reactions were out of all proportion to our concern for our friends.

In prayer, the Lord reminded me of a scene at home. It was the morning after the first night my dad had been away from home overnight. My mum had told me to ask him where he had been. When I asked, he replied by saying,

'What does it matter, nobody cares anyway.' I remember standing there with tears streaming down my face saying, 'But I care'. There was no-one to help me in my distress. My mum was in the kitchen. My dad was locked in his own pain and my brother was reading a newspaper, oblivious to all that was going on.

I felt my parents owed me a secure childhood as well as a secure home. Also I felt owed appreciation for me being me, and not just because of my academic achievements. There was also a lot of grief in my heart. I realised that not only had I lost a home, but I lost a mother and father too. At first, I tried to rationalise it all and 'let them off' because it was all understandable. But I finally realised that I was owed by both my parents, and that they could never repay me. Unless I wished to continue being robbed of my zest for life and being tormented by the pain in my shoulder, I knew I had to forgive them and release them from the debt.

The result has been that I feel like I have a new heart. I now have so much more energy and vitality. I have not been seriously ill since ... before this, I was off work every three months. I now have a wonderful baby which I can cope with. Before, I had to go to sleep on weekend after-noons, just to cope with a week's work. It is only through having forgiven and released my own dysfunctional family, that I can understand and help the broken and hurting families I see as a Child Psychiatrist.

Hope of approval disappointed

I was brought up in a reasonably normal home background. My dad was a teacher and so had long holidays with us. He was great fun and was always making something for us out of odd and ends. I remember how, when getting home from school, he would give us a big hug and a kiss. He was a great encourager and tried to bring the best out in us.

As he was a sports teacher, we would often go to watch him referee for the school team on a Saturday morning. He was also a Football League referee. This meant that on

Saturday afternoons, he would often be officiating at a league game somewhere. This was always exciting and occasionally we got to meet a famous player. During the game I would keep quiet, especially when the supporters started swearing at the ref!

As I got older I developed my own interests that were not sporty at all. In my early teens I became a Christian. At that time, three things became really important to me – music, electronics and my place in the church. My dad wasn't 'into' any of these things. Because I had experienced so much approval and encouragement in my younger years, I supposed it would continue when I was older. Sadly this was not the case.

It was not that he disapproved of my interests, but his almost neutral state made me feel like he did. Rationally, these three areas were out of his own experience. I supposed that he didn't know 'how' to encourage me in them. However I did feel hurt when he would make really positive comments to me about my brothers achievements, and seemingly little about my own.

In a time of prayer God showed me that as a result of this lack of approval in my teens, I had sought it elsewhere. Even in my twenties, anyone who looked remotely like a 'father figure' became a potential source of approval and appreciation for me. This was not good news for them, though. They couldn't give me what I was really looking for. The more I tried to get it, the more I felt discouraged and disapproved of!

God showed me that I needed to forgive and release my dad for the times I had expected and needed his approval in my teens and didn't get it. It was quite a painful experience. I had to ask God's forgiveness for seeking that approval elsewhere when I could have got it from Him.

Since then, I have felt free from the need to be approved of by my dad. If it comes it's a bonus! If it doesn't, I know that I have now found true security in relationship with my heavenly Father.

Zero emotions

I was brought up in a unhappy family setting. My Dad gave me no physical affection, vocal encouragement or approval. There was little or no communication between members of our family and certainly none on an emotional level. This background shaped my character and was to create a fertile environment for later issues.

I became a Christian in my early teens and although this gave me a relationship with God it did nothing for my underlying needs. Consequently I spent much of my teenage years searching for affection and affirmation in a series of relationships with girls.

I found it very difficult to share about myself on anything but a superficial level. I had no role model. This caused major problems in my subsequent marriage and role as a father. I did not know how to give myself or share my feelings. I dealt with everything on a logical, mental basis, neatly packaging away issues rather than dealing with them emotionally.

When I got baptised in the Holy Spirit there was a great change in areas of my character but emotions were still shut down in certain areas. I was unable to be hurt or feel pain emotionally for myself. Of course I did not recognise anything was wrong. This was just how I was – my normal self, or so I thought. I even counted being able to package things away as one of my strengths. How wrong I was.

God began to highlight the problems I had in my marriage so I sought help. It was during a time of ministry that God showed me that the problems lay in a relationship I had had in my midteens. She was my first love, the only person I had ever opened myself up to. I vividly remembered one particular day. Everything now flooded back. I was there again. This girl had told me she wanted to break up. I cried and cried until there were no more tears. I was deeply hurt and from that point my emotion died, I was not to be open with anyone again.

The reality that she had screwed up 17 years of my life, leaving me emotionally dead, needed sorting. I prayed, forgiving her for hurting me, for breaking my trust and destroying my openness. I released her from every debt she owed me.

Following ministry in which the emotional and mental strongholds were smashed down, I found my emotions began to function. This was very difficult for me, I felt so vulnerable. Things people said and did began to hurt me. These normal emotional responses to most people were unfamiliar to me. Many other areas from the past opened up. Emotions from times when I should have been hurt but was unable to feel the pain began to surface.

There were particular problem areas in my marriage which surfaced. This made me feel very insecure and hurt. God helped us to talk openly about the issues which was very difficult at first. We were then able to forgive and release each other. This has brought a freedom in my emotions and my marriage that I did not think possible, a whole new level of communication has developed.

It has been difficult learning to respond with normal emotions but I know that I have received considerable healing in my emotions. My marriage has been strengthened and our relationship has deepened.

Forgiving and releasing has opened up many areas which have been difficult to cope with and handle, but it has been the key to unlocking many closed areas of my life. This has had dramatically positive affects on the quality of my life and marriage.

Appendix A

How to Become a Christian

There are many different ways of explaining how to become a Christian. However, the New Testament presents three specific commands to those who want to enter into a relationship with God.

1. Repent!

We read in chapter 5 that Jesus was anointed and commissioned to:

> '...*preach the gospel ... proclaim release to the captives ... to set free those who are downtrodden ... to proclaim the favorable year of the Lord.*' (Luke 4:18f)

When Jesus began to preach he said,

> '...*Repent, for the kingdom of heaven is at hand.*'
> (Matthew 4:17)

In Acts 2, the Jews' response to hearing that Jesus was Lord, was to call out, 'What shall we do?' Peter's reply was

> '*Repent...*' (Acts 2:38)

To repent means to have a radical change in attitude towards God and sin. A person must be ruthlessly honest about their sin before God. Repentance is a determined **turning away from wrong**. It is not an 'optional extra' when becoming a Christian; it's a command to be obeyed. It is also the first component of a solid foundation for a person's spiritual life (Hebrews 6:1).

2. Believe!

Having been confronted by God's power shaking his prison, Paul's jailer asked,

> '"Sirs, what must I do to be saved?" And they said, "Believe in the Lord Jesus, and you shall be saved."'
>
> (Acts 16:30f)

The apostle Paul also said:

> 'Now I make known to you, brethren, the gospel which I preached to you, which also you received, in which also you stand, by which also you are saved, if you hold fast the word which I preached to you, unless you *believed* in vain.
>
> For I delivered to you as of first importance what I also received, that Christ died for our sins according to the Scriptures, and that He was buried, and that He was raised on the third day according to the Scriptures,
>
> (1 Corinthians 15:1–4)

What was it the jailer had to believe?

> '... that Christ died for our sins according to the Scriptures, and that He was buried, and that He was raised on the third day.'

To believe, the jailer had to **turn to God**, and put his faith in Jesus and make Him Lord (that means 'Boss'). He had to believe that Jesus died for him personally.

Jesus bore the punishment of the whole world's sin, when He died on the Cross.

> '... Christ was sacrificed once to take away the sins of
> many people; and he will appear a second time, not to
> bear sin, but to bring salvation to those who are waiting
> for Him.'   (Hebrews 9:28)

A person must not only believe that Jesus died for them,
but that He rose again from the dead.

> '... if you confess with your mouth Jesus as Lord, and
> believe in your heart that God raised Him from the
> dead, you shall be saved; for with the heart man
> believes, resulting in righteousness, and with the mouth
> he confesses, resulting in salvation.'   (Romans 10:9f)

3. Be Baptised!

> 'And Peter said to them, "Repent, and **let each of you be
> baptized in the name of Jesus Christ** for the forgiveness
> of your sins;'   (Acts 2:38)

Some time later, Peter preached the gospel to non-Jews.
Look what happened as he preached:

> '"Of Him all the prophets bear witness that through His
> name everyone who believes in Him receives forgive-
> ness of sins." While Peter was still speaking these
> words, the Holy Spirit fell upon all those who were
> listening to the message. And all the circumcised
> believers who had come with Peter were amazed,
> because the gift of the Holy Spirit had been poured out
> upon the Gentiles also. For they were hearing them
> speaking with tongues and exalting God. Then Peter
> answered, "Surely no one can refuse the water for these
> to be baptized who have received the Holy Spirit just as
> we did, can he?" And **he ordered them to be baptized** in
> the name of Jesus Christ...'   (Acts 10:43–48)

Peter did not give them the option of being baptised in water 'if they felt ready'. He saw evidence of their repentance and faith in that the Holy Spirit had been poured out on them. He **ordered** them to be baptised. This was in obedience to Jesus' command to his disciples in Matthew 28:19f,

> *'And Jesus came up and spoke to them, saying, "All authority has been given to Me in heaven and on earth. Go therefore and make disciples of all the nations, baptizing them in the name of the Father and the Son and the Holy Spirit, teaching them to observe all that I commanded you; and lo, I am with you always, even to the end of the age."'*

The word baptise means to dip, immerse or submerge. Figuratively, it means to overwhelm.

> *'And as they went along the road they came to some water; and the eunuch said, "Look! Water! What prevents me from being baptized?" And he ordered the chariot to stop; and they both went down into the water, Philip as well as the eunuch; and he baptized him. And when they came up out of the water, the Spirit of the Lord snatched Philip away; and the eunuch saw him no more, but went on his way rejoicing.'* (Acts 8:36, 38f)

When Philip the evangelist **preached Jesus** to the Ethiopian eunuch, he must have told him that the correct response should be to be baptised. Notice that they both went down into the water.

The Greek scholar, W.E. Vine says, 'baptism is the process of immersion, submergence and emergence.' Baptism is the correct biblical response to those who have repented and believed.

If you want to become a Christian, you must
>Repent of your sin
>Believe in the Lord Jesus

and in response to Jesus' command

    Be baptised in water.

You will certainly need help in getting baptised. Here is a prayer that you could pray by yourself right now, if you want to express your repentance and faith in Jesus.

> Lord Jesus, I know I have sinned and I am truly sorry. I repent and turn from living 'my way'. I turn my life over to you. Thank you that you died on the Cross for me and were punished for my sin. Please forgive me for my sin and cleanse me from it. Release me from the debts I owe you. Come into my life and take control as my Lord. As you have forgiven and released me, I will forgive and release those who have offended me.

In the book of Acts, Chapter 1, Jesus spoke about the Holy Spirit:

> *'for John baptized with water, but you shall be baptized with the Holy Spirit not many days from now.'*

Verse 8 says

> *'but you shall receive power when the Holy Spirit has come upon you; and you shall be My witnesses both in Jerusalem, and in all Judea and Samaria, and even to the remotest part of the earth.'*

The Holy Spirit came upon the disciples on the Day of Pentecost.

> *'And when the day of Pentecost had come, they were all together in one place. And suddenly there came from heaven a noise like a violent, rushing wind, and it filled the whole house where they were sitting. And there appeared to them tongues as of fire distributing them-selves, and they rested on each one of them. And they were all filled with the Holy Spirit and began to speak*

with other tongues, as the Spirit was giving them utter-ance.' (Acts 2:1–4)

Remember Acts 10? The Holy Spirit was poured out there also. The 'believers' also spoke with tongues. God has not changed! He is still pouring out the Holy Spirit on those who believe. Look what Peter said in Acts 2:28

'*... Repent, and let each of you be baptized in the name of Jesus Christ for the forgiveness of your sins; and* **you shall receive the gift of the Holy Spirit**. *For the promise is for you and your children, and for all who are far off, as many as the Lord our God shall call to Himself.'*

You are part of the '*all who are far off*' he was talking about.

Therefore, the promise of the Holy Spirit is for you too. You can be baptised in the Holy Spirit in the same way as the believers in Acts 2 and Acts 10 were. Do you remember that the word baptise figuratively means to overwhelm? To be baptised in the Holy Spirit means to be overwhelmed by the Holy Spirit. You can open yourself up to God the Holy Spirit right now. Ask him to come and fill your life.

Talk to someone you know who is a committed Christian. They should be able to help you further, and encourage you in your relationship with God.

Appendix B

If you have found this book helpful, you may want to copy the following pictures and keep them in your Bible. When you come to share with someone about forgiveness, they can be a useful visual aid.

```
Fruit

Seed


≈≈≈≈≈≈≈≈≈≈≈≈≈≈≈≈≈≈≈≈≈≈≈≈≈≈≈≈≈≈≈≈≈≈
Soil
                        Root
```

Root, Fruit, Seed and Soil

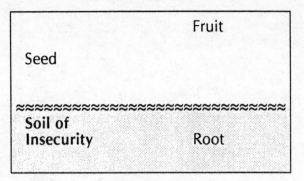

The Soil of Insecurity

Resulting from lack of
– acceptance,
– affirmation,
– appreciation,
– encouragement and
– love.

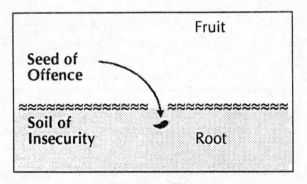

The Seed of Offence

– What others said
– What others didn't say
– What others did
– What others didn't do

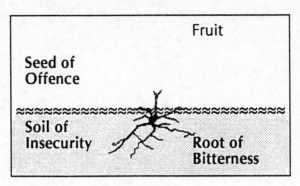

The Root of Bitterness

- What you think
- What you feel

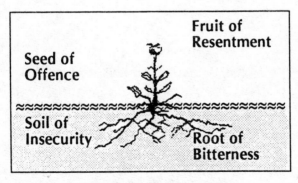

The Fruit of Resentment

- What you say
- What you do